Haunted Houses
and Wandering Ghosts
of California

Haunted Houses and Wandering Ghosts of California

by
Antoinette May

photography by
Ronald Shuman

A California Living Book

Also by Antoinette May

Haunted Ladies
Different Drummers

Cover Photo: Haskell House

First Edition

Copyright ©1977
The San Francisco Examiner Division of The Hearst Corporation.
Special Projects, Suite 911, The Hearst Building,
Third and Market Streets, San Francisco, California 94103.

Printed in the United States of America.

ISBN 0-89395-002-5

Library of Congress Catalog Card Number 77-92799

Dedication

To Nick Nocerino who never met a ghost he didn't like
and to C.J. Marrow who made the chase a very happy one.

Acknowledgments

My deepest appreciation to members of the Nirvana Foundation, the Nocerino research team, Psychic Science Investigators, and to June Reading and her staff at the Whaley House, for their invaluable assistance in the researching of this book.

Very special thanks to kindred spirits (live ones!) Ann Shotland, Roberta Ridgely and Marilyn Ferguson for the very best kind of support—moral, technical and practical.

But most of all to John Wilson, without whom this book would never have made it to the publisher.

Table of Contents

"I do not feel myself authorized to reject all ghost stories; for however improbable one taken alone might appear, the mass of them taken together command some credence."

Immanuel Kant

"From Ghoulies and Ghosties
    and Tong-leggety Beasties
And things that Go Bump in the Night
Good Lord, Deliver Us!"

Scottish prayer

Introduction

When Dr. Marshall Renbarger moved into a new office in San Jose in 1974, he was delighted with the convenient Crown Avenue location.

Then strange things started happening.

First he heard bells, loud clanging bells reminiscent of a church. But there was no church. Next he began to sense that he was not alone—when he was alone. Finally he became aware of strange dark-robed men gliding silently about the office.

When he discovered that no one else heard or saw the things he was experiencing, Dr. Renbarger grew concerned.

"Maybe I'm going crazy," he confided to a friend. "Wait till I tell you what's happening around here!"

"Don't tell me. I'll tell you," the friend stopped him. "I'll be right over to see for myself."

Fortunately for Dr. Renbarger's peace of mind, his friend was Sylvia Brown, president of the Nirvana Foundation—a non-profit organization devoted to psychic research. Sylvia, an accomplished medium, immediately tuned into the situation without hearing any of Dr. Renbarger's experiences.

"Why, it's an old chapel!" she exclaimed. "I see a little Spanish style church with a lot of monks wandering around. They seem very happy here, they certainly won't harm you."

Sylvia later verified her impressions by consulting county records. During the early days of California history, a chapel stood on the spot which now accommodates Marshall Renbarger's office.

And that's only *one* ghost story.

In the past year or so of investigating alleged hauntings, I've discovered that, psychically speaking, California is loaded—and apparently always has been.

The events are most commonly connected with a particular space—usually a house. They consist of poltergeist activity—unexplained disturbances such as sounds, smells, the movement of objects or temperature changes—or hallucinatory experiences, such as seeing "ghosts."

The parapsychologists who investigate these stories believe that hauntings and poltergeist phenomena—if verifiable—indicate an untapped energy source and, more importantly, survival of the human soul.

In searching out potential haunts, human investigators may be drawn to Charles Addams Victorians with their long, dark corridors, widow's walks, dramatic staircases, etc. But the ghosts themselves show a profound indifference to such things.

The ghost, it seems, is concerned with *what* happened to him, not where it happened. In most accounts of hauntings, the spirit comes back to erase, re-enact, avenge or simply brood about some awful event or unfulfilled longing. The spirit of Manuela Girardin, for instance, is said to hover about the room of her ailing grandchildren. Mrs. Girardin fell sick and died while tending the children one hundred years ago. Visitors to the historic Stevenson house in Monterey frequently report glimpsing her ghostly form.

Another lingering spirit is said to be that of Juanita, lynched by a gang of angry Gold Rush miners in retaliation for her having killed a member of their band who'd raped her. The tragedy will never be forgotten as long as Juanita returns to haunt the Downieville bridge where she was hanged.

Other spirits seem inclined to continue in more comfortable earthly patterns. What a devoted homemaker Anna Whaley must have been if in death she still returns to her home in San Diego just to check on things!

That California with its riotous history and unresolved conflicts would inspire a legion of restless spirits is not surprising. Even before statehood, Californians talked of a phantom cow, an apparition that wandered Yerba Buena Island, mooing mournfully over the loss of its calf, which had been barbecued by pirates. During Gold Rush days Mark Twain wrote of his encounter with the Kearny Street ghost, an apparition that confronted many early San Franciscans.

In December 1871, several thousand curious people flocked to another San Francisco location—the widow Jorgenson's house on Mason Street—where a bodiless head appeared at a second story window. The floating visage manifested itself at random day or night.

Reporters described a sorrowful face with a goatee, droopy mustache and longish, wavy hair. Though Mrs. Jorgenson disagreed, many felt that it resembled her late husband. Eventually the whole window was removed and taken for observation to a judge's office. The face followed. Later both were acquired by Woodward's Gardens, a popular restaurant. After a time the phantom face simply faded away.

Soon after, a group of poker players, gathered at the home of J. J. Hucks, looked up from their game to see another floating face—this time an elderly man with a long, bulbous nose—peering at them through an upper story window. Hucks walked fearlessly to the window and yanked down the shade. Apparently rebuffed, the specter did not return.

A more recent example of the same phenomenon was investigated in 1975 by PSI (Psychic Science Investigators), a group of researchers based in Fullerton.

PSI was called in when the visage of a Neanderthal-like man appeared in the mirror of a camp trailer parked in the Tahoe area. What is it? Where did it come from? Why did it appear? Nobody is quite sure. Members of the research team were able to successfully photograph the image which remains on the mirror today—despite numerous attempts to remove it.

PSI organized in 1973 to investigate psychic phenomena and has since visited literally hundreds of houses, museums and graveyards. Much evidence has been collected including a tape made at the San Juan Capistrano Cemetery of a voice that whispers breathily, "I want to give you my name." Another tape recorded message from a graveyard seance says quite distinctly, "I'm scared."

Antoinette May and Nick Nocerino

5

Sylvia Brown

Though the spirits may be frightened, the researchers definitely are not. Harry Shepherd, a leader of the group, speaks casually of a band of spirits who have seemingly attached themselves to his family. "I see them at night around the bed just as I drop off," he says. "There are five of them and if I don't see them all just before dozing off, I know that something's wrong. One night I noticed that one was missing and got up to check the house. Sure enough—a gas burner had been left on."

Not long after forming PSI, Chris and Norm Metzner became aware of "Fred," a spectral roommate whose reactions are very much of this world. Using a pasteboard box or card table as a means of demonstrating energy, the spirit responds visibly to the clink of glasses or the presence of a pretty woman. This entity responds to human encouragement and has been known to lift a table completely off the floor in full view of twenty people.

Probably the best known psychic investigator in California is F. R. "Nick" Nocerino, who has been involved in paranormal research for more than thirty years. A gifted medium, Nocerino has the ability to actually photograph spirits. Among the hundreds of pictures he has taken are blobs, lightning-like bolts or shafts of white light, and actual faces and forms of what appear to be discarnate entities. Some of the images are clear and distinct, while others are vague outlines. In some as yet unexplained way, Nocerino is able to act as a catalyst between the spirit or energy form and the light-sensitive film.

To take his extraordinary pictures, Nocerino uses an ordinary camera, a Pentax Honeywell with Tri-X 400 ASA film and no light. "I try to forget about the mechanics of picture taking," he says, "and just shut off my conscious mind. What I get in the picture is sheer energy—spirit energy." In accompanying Nick on some of his field trips, I've observed him take pictures of "things" invisible to the naked eye while at other times his camera was unable to photograph a phantom "light show" seen by many. This paradox seems common to all psychic photographers.

Nocerino has responded to thousands of requests for investigation—and sometimes exorcism—of reportedly haunted houses. Photographing the premises is an integral part of the investigation. Packaged film is unsealed on the spot and later developed commercially.

Of course all the ordinary explanations for apparent spirit photography are considered: faulty equipment, double exposure, light leaks or reflections, faulty development, refractions and, naturally, the possible delusion of the viewer. Any or all of these could account for the "spirit." After discounting for these possibilities, some pictures remain that can only be explained in supernatural terms.

Dr. Jules Eisenbud, clinical professor of psychiatry at the University of Colorado Medical School, says that since 1861 more than two dozen persons in several countries have claimed to obtain on photographic plates and film a variety of types of images that could only have been produced paranormally. I would tend to place the figure much higher.

How might such apparitions—on film or otherwise—be created? The most intriguing explanation is delayed telepathy. Assume that one experiences a severe shock such as witnessing or receiving word of a death. Immediately an image is created which may be intense enough to cause it to be "set" in time at a particular wavelength. Possibly years later, an individual whose receiver is tuned to the same wavelength is confronted with that image—and a ghost is born.

Judging from the number of individuals reporting spectral contact, one doesn't have to be a professional medium to see a ghost. They attract believer and nonbeliever indiscriminately. What seems to be required is the ability to tune into the electromagnetic field or "vibes." How many may have the ability to do this without even being aware of it?

To be a ghost hunter one needs only a rational outlook, a good memory, a sense of humor and an inquisitive, flexible mind. Basic equipment begins with a notebook and pencil—tape recorders, thermometers, cameras and geiger counters to be acquired as interest increases.

If nothing paranormal occurs while you are visiting the houses described here, you will have lost nothing. As an adventure in historical research, haunted houses have no equal.

As for the phenomenon of haunting itself, there's certainly nothing new about it. Ghost stories were popular in Roman times. Pliny wrote about spirits nearly two thousand years ago and there is indication that cave dwellers decorated their walls with pictures of them.

In the 16th Century, the Emperor Maximillian of Austria called out the army to ensure that there would be no ghosts in the hotels in which he planned to stay. Some two hundred years later Dr. Samuel Johnson observed to his friend and biographer, James Boswell, "It is wonderful that six thousand years have now elapsed since the creation of the world and still it is undecided whether or not there has ever been an instance of the spirit of any person appearing after death. All argument is against it, all belief is for it."

Recently 17,000 persons were queried by the British Society for Psychical Research. In answer to the question, "Have you ever, when believing yourself to be completely awake, had a vivid impression of seeing or being touched by a being or inanimate object, or of hearing a voice which was not due to any physical cause?" nearly 1700, or 10 per cent, answered YES.

Perhaps the strongest explanation for the ghost's continued popularity is its implied optimism. A spirit has literally conquered death and come back to prove it. It is both a clue and an invitation to a world beyond our own limited reality, an offer to broaden our awareness to encompass everything and anything that just might be possible.

And who can ignore that kind of challenge?

Antoinette May
Palo Alto, California

Master Ghost Chasers At Work

Barry Taff and Kerry Gaynor would like to shed some new light on an old subject—how to catch a ghost.

So far the way has not been easy. Once Barry's fountain pen was stolen by a ghost. Another time he was nearly strangled to death by a possessed subject. Once eight people watched in horror as a fifteen pound flower pot was suddenly levitated to the ceiling and then dumped with force enough to kill directly between the two researchers.

But far more shocking was the fate of their prize subject, "Mrs. B" of Culver City, who says she was raped by three spirits. Not too surprisingly, the B family had reached the point of desperation when the psychic research team was called in from the Neuropsychiatric Institute on the UCLA campus. The group is headed by Barry Taff, a parapsychologist with a Ph.D. in psychophysiology, and Kerry Gaynor, a recent UCLA graduate.

Mrs. B, a divorcee in her mid-thirties, lived in a dilapidated house which had twice been condemned by the city. Her family consisted of herself, a six-year-old daughter and three sons, ages ten, thirteen and sixteen. All described a particular apparition they called "Mr. Whose-it," which appeared to them in solid form and was just over six feet tall. Mrs. B and her eldest son had also seen two other entities, solid figures with oriental faces who appeared in Mrs. B's bedroom.

The B family emphatically dismissed the theory that the figures might have been imagined—they were far too vivid for that. Mrs. B told of being sexually assaulted by the three beings on several occasions and had bruises to prove it.

During their ten-week investigation of the house, the research team was frequently aware of intense cold spots and the strong, sometimes overpowering smell of decomposing flesh in Mrs. B's bedroom. Both the stench and cold spots faded in and out at random, sometimes disappearing completely. A thorough examination of the house offered no explanation.

One evening while Kerry was talking to the older son in the kitchen, a lower cabinet suddenly swung open and a pan flew out following a curved path before crashing to the floor nearly three feet from the cabinet.

On more than twenty occasions during the investigation, the team—which sometimes numbered as many as twenty researchers—witnessed a spectral light show which had an expanding, contracting appearance sometimes encompassing Mrs. B's entire bedroom.

In order to rule out the possibility of outside influences —reflections from street lights, passing cars, etc.—causing the lights, heavy quilts and bedspreads were placed over the windows. This seemed to have no effect upon the light show which now appeared even more brilliantly against darkened surroundings.

Mrs. B's son told the team that his Black Sabbath and Uriah Heep records seemed to infuriate the spirit. Reaction seemed particularly strong when the themes dealt with devil worship. As an experiment, the records were played in the presence of the group and the light activity dramatically increased, reaching a crescendo that appeared to match the feverish pitch of the music.

One evening it became apparent to the twenty researchers present that the lights were responding to provocative remarks made by Mrs. B. "In fact," Barry says, "when Mrs. B began to swear at the lights, assuming that they were in some manner related to the entities that attacked her, the lights intensified beyond all previous displays. It almost seemed as if the lights were the direct product of Mrs. B's psychic state, peaking and dipping in accordance with her emotional fluctuations."

One of the most interesting events of the evening involved the use of a geiger counter. As the lights reached peak intensity, the registration of background radiation—

previously constant—suddenly dropped to zero. When the light activity began to dwindle, fade and finally stop, the geiger counter's meter returned to its normal level of background radiation.

At the next session the lights began to take shape, forming the partial three dimensional image of a man whose shoulders, head and arms were readily discernible by each of the twenty individuals present.

Despite the battery of cameras clicking steadily away during these sessions, almost nothing of the light show was picked up on film. Yet another night when nothing was happening lightwise, Barry photographed a small ball of light that no one had seen.

"I took the picture on an impulse," he explains. "A sudden rush of cold current and a pervasive stench seemed to flow from the closed bedroom door. I shot the picture in the hall, seemingly of a wall and a closed door. Though none of us saw anything, the camera recorded a ball of light about a foot in diameter."

During the three month period of investigation the phenomena seemed to intensify. Mrs. B told of being chased by a pair of candelabra which took off from the kitchen sink and flew across the room—a distance of some twelve feet—and struck her arm. The group examined her large, red bruise.

Mrs. B's twelve-year-old son, who witnessed the event, said that the flying candelabra barely missed him. The B's also told Barry that a large wooden board which had been nailed to the wall beneath one of the bedroom windows was torn loose from its secured position as if by unseen hands and propelled some fifteen feet across the room, narrowly missing the boy's head before falling harmlessly to the floor.

In an effort to escape the phenomena, the B family moved to a new home. For a time this appeared to passify the forces which seemed to delight in persecuting them—but not for long. They are besieged again. Who is

it? What is it? Taff and Gaynor believe the evidence gives every indication of a discarnate intelligence and have recommended an exorcism.

Taff and Gaynor became involved in another equally bizarre case when two men employed in the UCLA photo lab told them of a party they'd attended where "books just flew around by themselves."

Not your typical Hollywood party, they agreed and went on to check out the house. What they found was a charming Spanish Colonial, vintage 1921, with a romantic past—Barbara Stanwyck and Robert Taylor once lived there. The owner, Don Jolly, a senior vice president of a savings and loan company, admitted that strange things did happen about the place. Only the week before his houseboy had quit, complaining that cabbages had chased him about the house.

On May 14, 1976 Taff and Gaynor returned to Jolly's home in the Hollywood hills with a KTTV news team. Almost immediately an ice tray flew from the kitchen and crossed the dining room where it crashed against a far wall. Next a large shower head from an upstairs bathroom floated through the livingroom where it finally fell to the floor in full view of fifteen people.

While standing in the bar area, Don Jolly and Barry were pelted by a shower of coins which appeared to fall from the empty air. Coasters took off from the dining room table soaring into the livingroom and a large sack of napkins flew out of the kitchen into the dining room followed by a large, heavy pewter goblet which struck the wall with enough force to rip off the plaster.

The outside of the house proved equally hazardous. Richard Matheson, Jr., a member of the news team, was nearly hit on the head by a flying shoe as he searched the grounds.

Newscaster Connie Fox, hoping to escape the flying objects inside, ran out onto the front porch only to be chased by a World Book Atlas that intercepted her on the walkway and chased her down the front stairs. (In order to accomplish this, the Atlas had to make three distinct turns, as the walkway of the hillside home is constructed in a Z-shape.) Members of the team who witnessed the event said that the pursuing book was almost birdlike as it flapped its pages.

Barry noted that the electricity within the house seemed to turn itself on and off at will throughout the evening, selectively negating specific circuits. Whenever the KTTV crew attempted to film in the house, their power was cut off while other circuits were unaffected. Even battery powered equipment such as tape recorders and electronic camera flashes refused to function. The street lamp directly in front of Jolly's house was affected, though the other street lights on the block continued to glow.

No one was too surprised when Don Jolly sold the house just three months later.

The most mysterious case ever investigated by the team was the Trafton home in Pacific Palisades. It began when Bliss Trafton, a young school teacher, approached Barry one evening at UCLA. "You're going to think I'm crazy when I tell you this, but there's a ghost dressed in armor who walks around our house at night." She went on to describe the almost ordinary—to Barry—cold spots and objects that moved from room to room of their own volition.

Taff went out to investigate the house and almost immediately lost a prize pen. "It was a rather expensive pen," he says, "distinguished by a bent clip and silver ornamentation—it couldn't be mistaken for another. I'd hardly set it down on the coffee table in front of me before it disappeared. I'd only been in the room a few seconds, my pen and notebook sitting there before me. Then when I went to pick up my pen, it was gone.

"Of course we looked under the furniture thinking that it might have rolled off—but it hadn't. No one had left the room, no one had picked it up without my noticing. The pen simply wasn't there. Finally we just gave up and went on with the investigation. A few minutes later I found my pen in a rear bedroom of the house. How do you explain that one?"

During the visit, Barry and his team experienced the same cold spots and pounding noises that the Trafton family had described.

A surprising postscript occurred a few months later when the Traftons decided to add on to the rear of their home. While digging the foundation, workmen uncovered graves containing skeletons dressed in armor of the type worn by the Spanish conquistadors.

Barry Taff considers his most fascinating haunting to have occurred in Inglewood. It's the only case where he's personally encountered direct malevolent activity. The manifestations began, he says, with apparitions of deceased prior occupants. Many of the neighbors who didn't know that the former owners were dead continued to see them at their daily chores about the house and grounds.

On several occasions individuals inside the house saw a variety of objects being flung about or floating through the air. Doors and windows opened and closed of their own accord and the sounds of a man walking about the house were heard. They also noticed that a display case remained dust free as if it were being polished daily while other pieces of furniture in the unoccupied house were heavily laden with dust.

"The results of a seance conducted in the house were startling to everyone—but nearly fatal to me," Barry says. "As some twenty people watched, one of the sitters—the grandson of a deceased prior occupant of the house—became violent and suddenly attacked me. The man's actions were like one possessed. 'Get out of my house! This is my house!' he seemed to snarl as his fingers tightened about my throat. It took five large men to drag him off me—they had to knock him unconscious to do it. When the man came to, he had no recollection of what had happened. His last memory was of *someone* saying 'Get out of my house.'

"During the attack by the twenty-five-year-old man, the others present didn't see *him* attack me. Instead they saw an older, larger, white haired man.

"The attack broke up the evening. The next day I received a call from a neighbor. He claimed to have seen the old man out in the yard and had heard the sounds of something being smashed inside the house.

"Upon our return the next evening, we observed that all the furniture with the exception of the well-dusted display case had been thrown to the floor. The house was littered with broken glass and almost every drawer had been pulled out and its contents strewn about the floor.

"It should be noted that the grandson who attacked me elected to subject himself to intensive psychological testing in order to determine whether he had a latent capacity for unprovoked violence of this degree. His psychiatric and psychological profile indicated that there was no such tendency.

"I could only conclude from this that his mind and body had somehow been seized by the grandfather who for his own reasons resented my presence in the house.

"What does it all mean? We began our investigation hoping to explain ghosts or explain them away. Seven years later, we can do neither. My search remains where it began. I can only explain haunting as I did at the beginning: a *phenomenon*. Maybe the next house . . . ."

San Diego Area

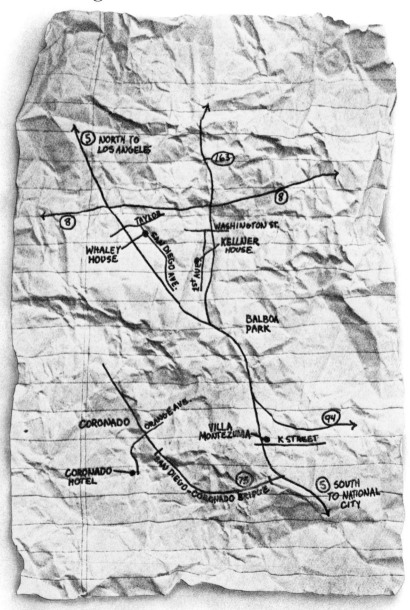

The Thomas Whaley House

Funeral humor occupies a very special place within the human consciousness. No matter how sophisticated the culture or the individual, the need remains to render death less fearful with a little tentative ridicule. Perhaps laughter is itself an affirmation of life. Macabre jokes are always in vogue.

A perennial favorite is the one about the boy who disrupts mourners at a burial service by rushing about crying, "Programs! Programs! Get your programs! You can't tell the dead ones from the live ones without a program!"

For June Reading, director of the historic Whaley House in San Diego (2482 San Diego Avenue) the problem of determining the live ones is no joke. After twenty years in a haunted house, she takes the apparitions that inhabit the showplace in her stride—though, admittedly, it's confusing to see someone wandering about and not know whether he or she is a living ticket holder or a spectre from the original cast.

Current fashions only add to the confusion. That exotic dark-haired woman standing before the bench in a flamboyant outfit could be the spirit of a fandango girl hauled into court—when the Whaley House doubled as a courthouse—for hustling too aggressively. Those two young girls fluttering about the upstairs bedroom in their gingham granny gowns might be the Whaley daughters who once caused the house to echo with the sound of their treadle sewing machine. And that tall, mustachioed man in a dark coat and vest standing at the top of the stairs, couldn't that be Thomas Whaley himself?

June Reading has sometimes thought so.

The Whaley House, built in 1857, was once the grand mansion of a frontier town. The very walls seem charged with passion, violence, fear and anger, rendered even more impressive by the knowledge that the house was built on a site used for public executions. How much

June Reading

unfinished business still remains can only be judged by the number of restless spirits seen by visitors and caretakers and by the frequency of their appearances.

The story of Thomas Whaley, the man who built the house, is—in part—the saga of San Diego itself. He was the son of an early America pioneer family grown to prosperity, and a life of conventional ease at the helm of the family business in New York seemed to stretch before him like a plush Victorian carpet. Then a stray headline caught his eye. It was the year 1848. A tea caddy of nuggets had been presented to President Polk, glittering evidence of gold in California.

At twenty-five, young Whaley was ripe for adventure, eager to make his own way in an exciting new world. He was among the first wave of adventurers to reach California, focusing on commerce rather than mining.

During the extremely hazardous 204-day voyage around Cape Horn, the young man's thoughts were of the sweetheart he'd left behind. Writing home to his mother, he suggested, "You might call on Mrs. De Lannay; you will find her a very pleasant lady. I may as well inform you that I have a particular regard for her youngest daughter, Miss Anna; indeed I love her and intend marrying her if I ever return from California a rich man."

Growing impatient, he added, "I may send for her. She is a pleasant and amiable young lady of very affectionate disposition and gentle and innocent as a lamb. She is only sixteen or seventeen years of age. You would no doubt love her as a daughter-in-law . . . ."

To Anna, he glowingly described a thriving village and nightly fandango dances but discreetly omitted the fact that San Diego was under marshal law as a result of frequent Indian attacks. Between battles, Thomas wrote, "Not a night passes, Anna, but that I look at your daguerrotype . . . I sleep with it under my pillow . . . It gives me great pleasure to gaze upon it . . . You may have grown

tall, become corpulent, and have adopted the 'Bloomer Costume' . . . If that were the case I should not know you . . . I am ready to take you for better or worse, so it makes no difference in what shape you appear so long as you come."

The courtship—conducted entirely by mail—lasted five years. Thomas returned to New York, married Anna and brought her back with him to San Diego. Soon he began construction of the home that would one day be known as the Whaley House. It was, he wrote home to mother, "the nicest place in San Diego." As the years passed many dignitaries enjoyed the hospitality of the Whaley home, including Presidents Grant and Harrison.

Later the county leased a portion of the home to be used as a courthouse for $65 a month. One large room was set aside for the courtroom and three upstairs rooms for storage of county records. Frontier justice was dispensed there for several years.

Then as new settlers began to pour into the area, the population of San Diego shifted from Old Town—where the Whaley House was located. New Towners became increasingly demanding, insisting that county offices and records be moved to a more central location. Whaley and other Old Town dignitaries stubbornly refused to yield. Finally an order was obtained to seize the records and county furniture.

Incensed, the people of Old Town announced that any effort to remove the records would be met with rifle fire. Once again marshal law was declared in Old Town. The Whaley House was sandbagged for protection and militant residents carried six-guns. "Old Town has seceded!" the San Diego Union announced in bold headlines following the placement of a cannon before the Whaley House.

Tensions lessened as no immediate effort was made to enforce the order. Whaley decided that it was safe to make a quick business trip to San Francisco. At midnight following his departure, the opposing forces greased their rented

Wells Fargo wagons, muffled their horses' hoofs with gunny sacks and headed for the Whaley House. There the armed party forced its way inside and stopped Anna at gunpoint on the ninth step of the stairway leading to the record storage room.

Hearing the sound of footsteps, six-year-old Lillian Whaley jumped out of bed believing that her father had returned home unexpectedly. Running to greet him, she was confronted by the sight of her tiny 4'11" mother surrounded by armed men. Though Lillian lived to be a very old woman, she never forgot the incident.

And neither would Whaley who was greeted by the accomplished fact upon his return a few days later. Learning that his beloved wife had been threatened, his castle invaded, and a goodly source of revenue removed, Whaley was furious. Indignantly, he penned numerous letters to the board demanding rent and repairs on the building which had been damaged by the break-in. The fact that the lease had not expired, leaving the county clearly liable, was blatantly ignored by everyone but Whaley. His requests that the action be reviewed were denied. Again and again his angry letters were "tabled for future consideration."

Though the glory years were over, the lusty pioneer had no intention of admitting defeat. He continued litigation until his death nineteen years later. The affair was never settled. Anna Whaley died in 1913; but Lillian, who had witnessed the dramatic scene as a small child, lived on in the family home until her own death in 1953—just nine days short of her ninetieth birthday.

In 1956 the Board of Supervisors of the County of San Diego vindicated itself to some degree by purchasing the then dilapidated dwelling which was slated for destruction. The house was restored and refurnished and is now maintained by the Historical Shrine Foundation.

But that's only the beginning of the story.

Almost immediately June Reading, who was active in directing the renovation of the home, was aware of some mysterious, unexplained presence. It began with footsteps. She recalls a morning when she arrived at the house early, intending to furnish the upstairs rooms. "Two men were with me," she explains. "They were county workmen who were painting some shelving in the hall. Suddenly we heard the distinct sound of someone walking in the bedroom above us. I assumed that it must be another workman who'd arrived ahead of us, but when I went up to investigate there was no one there. One of the men joked about spirits coming in to look things over and we promptly forgot the matter. That was such a busy time—the house was to be opened to the public in just one week.

"However, the sound of walking continued. And for the next six months I found myself going upstairs again and again to see if someone was actually there. This would happen during the day, sometimes when visitors were in other parts of the house, or at other times when I was busy at my desk trying to catch up on correspondence or bookwork. At times it would sound as if someone was descending the stairs, but the steps would fade away before reaching the first floor.

"The next thing we knew the windows in the upper part of the house began to assert themselves, opening seemingly of their own volition. We installed horizontal bolts on three windows in the front bedroom, thinking that would end the matter. It didn't. The really annoying part of it all came when the opening of the windows set off our burglar alarm in the middle of the night. Frequently we were called by the police and the San Diego Burglar Alarm Company, to come and see if the house had been broken into. Only once did we find any evidence of human disturbance."

In October 1962, while giving a talk to twenty-five school children, Mrs. Reading again heard the sound of someone walking. The footsteps seemed to come from the roof. After one of the children interrupted to ask what the noise was, she went outside to see if a county repairman might be working on the roof. There was no one in sight.

It soon came to light that residents of Old Town were familiar with this sound. It had been a neighborhood phenomenon for many years. Lillian Whaley had often complained of it during her long lifetime in the house. Neighbors also told of how a large, heavy china closet had tipped over seemingly of its own volition in 1912, one year before the death of Anna Whaley.

Before long a colorful parade of apparitions began to appear. Grace Bourquin, a volunteer guide at the house, looked up one afternoon and saw the figure of a man on the staircase, clad in a frock coat and pantaloons.

A Mrs. Kirby, wife of the Director of the Medical Association of New Westminster, B.C., who was visiting the house, saw an apparition of a woman in the courtroom. She described the woman as small and dark skinned, wearing a calico dress with a long full skirt reaching to the floor and gold hoops in her pierced ears. The spirit's eyes and hair were dark. "I get the impression that she lives here and we are sort of invading her privacy," the astonished tourist confided.

On November 28, 1963, Mrs. Suzanne Pere of El Cajon, California, reported seeing a kind of spectral town meeting. "There was a group of men in the study dressed in frock coats," she said. "One had a thick gold watch chain across his vest. It seemed to be a very lively discussion; all the figures were animated, some pacing the floor, others conversing; all serious and agitated, oblivious to everything else. One figure in the group seemed to be an official and stood off by himself. This person was of medium stocky build, had light brown hair, and a mustache which was quite full and long. He had very piercing light blue eyes and a penetrating gaze. He seemed about to speak."

Many who have visited the house have reported hearing deep, baritone laughter, smelling cologne and/or cigar smoke, and feeling pressure upon themselves while climbing the stairs as though something were trying to prevent their progress. One woman felt herself literally forced out of an upstairs bedroom by unseen hands.

In 1965 the famous English medium Sybil Leek was invited to visit the Whaley House in the hope that she might be able to make contact with its discarnate inhabitants. TV personality Regis Philbin and a camera crew were on hand to record the event. Disavowing any knowledge of the past history of the house—the trials of Thomas Whaley or the recent psychic disturbances—the medium, who had just flown in for the occasion, proceeded to communicate with a troubled male spirit who muttered resentfully of people in the house. Speaking through Sybil's lips, the entity told of an injustice perpetrated upon him and demanded redress.

The words coincided exactly with letters written ninety years before by Thomas Whaley which had never been placed on public display. When the spirit's angry harangue was played back via a tape recorder, the forceful intonations of the voice exactly matched the imprint of a quill pen at various obviously heated passages in the correspondence. Splashes of ink testified to the indignant emphasis of the writer coinciding exactly with the forceful exclamations of the speaker.

The spirit then told of opening the windows and triggering the alarm bell, thereby causing the police to come. This was a means of calling attention to himself, he explained, of showing the world that he was still master of the house. Sybil had not been given any of this background information, nor could she possibly have known the maiden name of Anna Whaley which was imparted to her by the spirit. "Anna Lannay plays the organ," she understood him to say.

Contact was also made with another spirit, one who complained of a bad fever, talked of "confusion" around him and begged for a drink of water. This manifestation was later related to a tragic occurrence which had taken

The spot where Yankee Jim was hung

place in 1852 when the land which would later accommodate the Whaley House was used as a place of execution. It involved a man by the name of Yankee Jim Robinson who had jumped ship and stolen a boat. The runaway sailor was merely rowing about the bay sightseeing when apprehended. In attempting to escape, Robinson was wounded in a sabre duel. This injury did not heal, and while languishing in jail, he became seriously ill. The unfortunate man was dragged into court while suffering from a raging fever and remained unconscious throughout much of the trial.

When the drunken judge pronounced sentence—death by hanging—Jim thought it was merely a bad joke intended to teach him a lesson. Dazed by his illness, he continued in this wishful thinking until the execution wagon was pulled from under him and he dangled from a rope. To add to the agony of the moment, the scaffold was too short for Yankee Jim's long legs. Instead of his neck being broken instantly, he was allowed to slowly strangle to death. The cruel death took forty-five minutes and was never forgotten by the witnesses who told of his anguished curses.

The scaffold had stood in the place where an archway now divides the music room of the Whaley House from the front parlor. Many consider this a cold, fearsome spot without knowing its gruesome history. In 1935, Lillian Whaley told a reporter from the *San Diego Union* that her father had once rented the house temporarily to tenants who were so frightened by the presence of Yankee Jim that they had the house exorcised.

One who claims to have seen Yankee Jim in recent times is Kay Sterner, a retired school teacher with psychic ability, who visited the house at the request of June Reading in 1968. Mrs. Sterner, who is founder-president of the California Parapsychology Foundation, knew nothing of the Whaley House or its previous occupants.

While approaching the house the gifted medium was suddenly aware of a primitive scaffold with a man hanging from it. A team of mules had just pulled a wagon from beneath the struggling body. The scene seemed to be superimposed on the house itself and Mrs. Sterner was able to point out that the spectral scaffold was erected on the site of the arch between the music room and the livingroom, a fact verified by county records.

Clairvoyantly, Kay Sterner was then able to "see" an old coach house—long since gone—and a wagon with two horses standing in the backyard. The description was later confirmed. In the courtroom inside the Whaley House, she saw a rowdy group of sailors, prostitutes and apparent bandits taking their turns before the bench. The atmosphere seemed charged with tension as they continued to replay some dramatic episode of more than one hundred years ago.

One of the most evidential of the sightings was that of a stocky man wearing boots and carrying a log book. He appeared to be disturbed and Mrs. Sterner picked up the fact that he was upset about a case that he had adjudicated. He was a highly scrupulous man, she said, and seemed to suffer from a leg injury.

June Reading later informed her that this description matched that of Squire A. R. Ensworth, who had been Whaley's lawyer and business manager, and also a magistrate. Mrs. Reading showed the medium letters indicating great concern on Ensworth's part as to whether he had made the right decision in a specific case involving Whaley. She also revealed that the lawyer had fallen into a hole on the property and broken his leg. It had never been properly set.

Even more dramatic was the re-enactment before the medium's very eyes of a brutal murder. The phenomenon began with loud, agonizing screams. Then she saw a Mexican woman with long flowing dark hair, a bright blouse and long ruffled skirt run shrieking down the hall. She was pursued by a dark complexioned man who accused her of being unfaithful. There was a violent quarrel and Kay Sterner watched in helpless terror as the man drew a knife and slashed his errant love to death. Later she learned from Mrs. Reading that a heated quarrel between a Mexican couple had ended with the wife's stabbing. The tragedy had occurred in the upstairs bedroom as the medium had seen it.

Another sad event witnessed by Mrs. Sterner and then verified by the historian was the death of a small child. The medium "saw" this taking place in the room where Tom Whaley had died at seventeen months.

The final apparition revealed clairvoyantly was that of a woman wearing a nightgown and cap making the rounds of the house, checking to see if the children were asleep, the windows fastened and the doors bolted. One might assume that Mrs. Whaley—like her husband—still holds a proprietary claim upon an earthly status symbol.

So much verifiable information coming from psychic sources does seem to corroborate the legends of the house as well as the current manifestations that seem all in a day's work to June Reading and her assistants. The years pass and the stories persist. The smell of Thomas Whaley's favorite cigar floats down the corridors, a ghostly gavel echoes, a rocker unaccountably begins to rock.

Twenty years have passed since the opening of the house as a museum. Now fresh history mingles with old. New wonder tales are collected as visitors suddenly catch glimpses of spirits who apparently find life in the Whaley House just too exciting to leave behind.

19

Rancho Jamul in the 1850's
Photo courtesy of the Historical Collection
of the Title Insurance and Trust

Rancho Jamul

Some historians believe the name "Jamul" meant water of the antelope. Some say it meant good water, while others insist that it is the ancient Indian word for slimy water.

But no matter what kind of water it was, there was plenty of it there in 1829 when Pio Pico received his 8,926 acre grant from the governor of California. It was a splendid windfall even for those open-handed times.

An imposing hacienda was built, cattle stocked, and before long the rancho was a showplace. Then in 1837, while Pico was away and his mother and three unmarried sisters were staying at the rancho, a half-breed servant warned the family that neighboring Indians were massing for attack. The Pico family fled; but their majordomo, Juan Leiva, remained with his family.

It was a tragic mistake. Leiva's son, Jose, was killed almost immediately by Indians as were the other vaqueros. Juan Leiva, though wounded, was able to stagger to the gun room just in time to see an Indian servant lock the door and run away. He was finally reduced to defending his family by flinging coals from the fireplace at the advancing savages.

His courageous stand was useless. Leiva was slaughtered; his wife, Dona Maria, and their young son were stripped and then abandoned in the wilderness. The proud Pico estate was set afire, the house totally destroyed. Dona Maria watched helplessly as her two teenage daughters were carried away by the Indians. She and her small son then walked the twenty-one miles to San Diego barefoot and naked.

An expedition was sent out to rescue the girls. The small but determined force searched for three months. Once the Indians were overtaken. The girls could be seen in the distance, their bodies smeared with white paint, their hair cut Indian fashion. Many were killed in the battle that followed but the surviving savages dragged the screaming girls back into the hills.

When the contingent returned to San Diego, Dona Maria was dead. The violent tragedy had simply proved too much for her. Though a large reward was offered for the recovery of the Leiva girls, they were never seen again.

And that's only one story connected with Rancho Jamul—now one of the largest cattle ranches in the state.

During the 1870's tragedy again erupted at Jamul. California was part of the United States now and many of the greedy newcomers felt that fact gave them precedence over the Spanish-speaking natives. Hordes of squatters descended upon the place.

The Mexican-American owners of Rancho Jamul took their claim to the Supreme Court and won, but that was not the end of their problems by any means. The squatters simply refused to budge.

Over the years the rancho was the scene of bloody feuds and a series of grisly unresolved murders—squatters found with their heads bashed in. According to one legend, the murderer was discovered and immediately lynched by an angry mob. When the authorities arrived, the body had disappeared. It was never found.

Generations of ranch hands at Jamul have told of apparitions, lights, cold spots, the cries of Indians and the screams of women. Some refuse to venture into certain areas of the sprawling ranch.

The second Pico home, built in 1852 and elegantly modernized in recent years, is owned today by Lawrence and Bertha Daley.

"People are always seeing things, hearing things," Bertha Daley says. "I often stay here alone but never *feel* alone. Whatever's here must like me and I certainly like it—or them. We have an understanding, I think—a mutual respect. The vicious tragedies of the past have left their imprint. One feels it, of course, but history is a continuing thing that unfolds from day to day. I feel the past. I'm aware of it every day, but I still live very much in the now."

Hotel del Coronado

The Hotel del Coronado (1500 Orange Avenue, Coronado) has been called a living legend. Archives remind us that it was built shortly after the death of General Custer—during the days when the infamous Black Bart roamed the state.

Presidents Harrison, McKinley, Taft, Wilson, Franklin D. Roosevelt, Kennedy, Johnson and Nixon have slept here.

The Prince of Wales, later King of England, met his future duchess at a gala hosted in his honor in the grand ballroom of the hotel. The date was April 7, 1920. The young prince was said to be "nuts" about dancing.

The same year a movie, *The Flying Fleet*, starring Ramon Navarro and Anita Page, was filmed in the Victorian manorhouse.

In 1958, Billy Wilder chose the hotel as a setting for *Some Like It Hot*, starring Marilyn Monroe, Tony Curtis, and Jack Lemmon. Marilyn Monroe, described by the help as a "sweet, quiet lady who ate her one daily meal alone in her room," was merely one superstar in a dazzling chain. Fifty years before, Sarah Bernhardt pronounced the place "Charmante!"

During the 1890s the hotel management proudly advertised,

> "There is not any malaria, hay-fever, sleeplessness, loss of appetite, or languor in the air; nor any thunder, lightning, mad dogs, cyclones, heated-terms or cold-snaps—and all these advantages may be enjoyed for $3.00 per day and upward."

Conspicuously absent was any mention of the hotel's resident ghost.

According to one legend, a young woman guest mysteriously disappeared from Room 502. But another story

has the woman committing suicide in that room. In that version, the owner, Elisha Babcock, fearing a scandal, secretly disposed of the corpse, never dreaming that the young lady would stubbornly refuse to check out.

Year after year her spirit remains, astonishing mortal guests with a variety of poltergeist activity. Doors and windows are said to open and close of their own volition. Footsteps are heard inside the seemingly empty room. Even though Babcock professed not to believe in such "nonsense," he wrote to his son that circumstances had forced him to seal the room.

The ghostly guest has outlasted five successive owners and continues her tenancy to this day. Marcie Buckley, an employee of the hotel since 1967, reports that other paying guests have frequently complained of un-expected noises and articles that "move about the room." John Wayne Godown, who works the front desk, tells of some who have demanded to be moved after one night in room 502.

Possibly for this reason, the room is rented only when every other accommodation is filled. Yet security guards roaming the twisting fifth floor corridors describe lights that suddenly turn on and off in the unoccupied room.

Besides the ghost, Room 502 boasts one window with a commanding view of the grand hotel's splendid Victorian cupola—in the closet. And another window that looks out into the hall.

To the hotel management this room may be the last resort, but excitement-wise, some guests have rated it quite high.

Villa Montezuma

Fakir or faker?

Jesse Shepard may have been either or both.

Whichever, whatever, the old enchantment still holds. Very few can remain immune once they've penetrated the fascinating forcefield surrounding Jesse's "villa."

City historians have described Villa Montezuma (1925 K Street, San Diego) as the finest example of Victorian architecture on the West Coast. But neighbors call it the "Spook House."

A brooding sentinel overlooking downtown San Diego, the house that Jesse built seems the perfect setting for a Gothic mystery tale.

And that's exactly what it is.

First there's the curse. Tragedy has stalked each successive owner for the past ninety years.

Then there's the treasure. A legend involving hidden treasure has tantalized and defeated decades of intriguers.

Finally there's the ghost. A servant, desolate over the death of his wife, is said to have hanged himself in the onion-shaped tower. Neighbors whisper that late at night his grief-ravaged face may be seen staring beseechingly from a window. Some tell of hearing piteous moans.

The legend had its beginning when Jesse Shepard appeared on the streets of San Diego in 1887, strikingly handsome, with the air of a matinee idol. Only one thing about Jesse is absolutely certain: he had a genius for timing. Here was a man at the right place at the right time doing the right thing.

The Atchison, Topeka and Santa Fe Railroad had recently linked San Diego to the east, triggering a wild flurry of real estate speculation. Land prices skyrocketed as 50,000 newcomers crowded into the little village, each determined to get rich fast.

Shepard stood out among the multitude, quickly carving a glittering niche for himself. He had already sung his way into the salons of Paris where his amazing vocal range—from base to soprano—had earned invitations to visit and entertain titled patrons throughout Europe.

Small wonder the Beautiful People of the day were impressed. Jesse could sing all the parts from any opera from memory—and as though that weren't enough—he could somehow manage to sing in two voices at the same time.

The French novelist Alexander Dumas was so turned on that he predicted: "With your gifts you will find all doors open before you."

Those doors were to include the portals of spiritualism as well. While entertaining in St. Petersburg, Jesse became the protege of the Czar's own medium, General Jourafsky. From that seer he learned to conduct seances. Later the great Helena Blavatsky put the fine edge on his mystical education.

Shifting his attention to San Diego, Shepard was quickly befriended by a pair of wealthy cattlemen, William and John High. One story is that the spirit of William's deceased wife instructed the two brothers to build a monument to her memory—with the details to be handled by Jesse.

Another more likely version is that the canny cattlemen, knowing a good thing when they saw it, perceived the drawing power of the charismatic Shepard. By bankrolling the singing spiritualist they ensured a lucrative future for themselves in land development. This theory seems born out by the fact that the High brothers immediately bought up all the property surrounding Shepard's house site and later resold it at a handsome profit.

San Diego watched the construction of the Shepard place with interest. It was readily apparent that this was to be no ordinary run-of-the-mill mansion. With its many turrets and a flaming onion-shaped tower topped by a flying devilfish flicking its tongue at the sky, it looked exactly like the temple of mysticism that it was soon to become.

James Shepard called his gingerbread palace Villa Montezuma. An evening there was literally an out-of-this-world experience. The place became a social mecca drawing not only San Diego society but visiting notables as well.

A special feature was the music room with its immense stained glass window from which the likeness of Jesse can be seen today gazing down in the guise of a crusader. The room is said to be haunted.

It was here that Shepard's musical seances were performed. Sitting in darkness, guests are said to have watched transfixed while Jesse clairaudiently received music from another world.

A highlight was the *Grand Egyptian March*—a musical miracle. Using only the piano and his own voice, it is said Jesse recreated the measured advance of two opposing armies. As a trumpet sounded "Charge!" the clash of cutlasses could be heard and the booming of cannons. Finally the sounds of battle—which seemed to come from walls, floor and ceiling—died away and only the piano could be heard.

What was left for an encore? In 1889 Jesse sold Villa Montezuma and returned to Europe. He would later die in poverty in a dingy Los Angeles hotel room. The mansion was also headed into a decline. The next owner, D. D. Dare, vice president of the California National Bank, was accused of looting the firm. A partner committed suicide. Dare fled one step ahead of the police.

The third owner, H. R. Palmerston, mortgaged the house, made a fatal investment and lost the property through foreclosure. The same fate awaited the next owners. Dr. George M. Calmus, his wife and mother-in-law lived for several years in the grand mansion until Calmus' unlucky investments brought him to bankruptcy. The shock affected his mind. He deserted his family, mysteriously disappearing and leaving the two women to face eviction alone.

The last private owner was Amelia Jaegar, a former silent film actress. Mrs. Jaegar lived in constant terror and carried a gun with her at all times. Eager to be rid of the accursed house, she sold it for half its value. The sale was later voided by the court on the grounds that Amelia Jaegar was of an unsound mind at the time of the transaction.

Against her will, Villa Montezuma was returned to her.

In 1972 the house passed into the hands of the City of San Diego and is administered now as a free museum by the San Diego Historical Society. Despite the no-nonsense official position of the city fathers, the ghostly legend of Jesse Shepard stubbonly refuses to fade. Visitors to the museum describe apparitions and spectral reflections suddenly glimpsed in the house's numerous mirrors. George Schicker, the Sunday tour guide, frankly admits to feeling Jesse's presence in the music room.

Others tell of another ghost, a tragic sobbing figure who haunts the upstairs rooms. This is believed to be the legendary moaner still mourning the passing of his wife.

It appears that a good ghost *can* fight City Hall.

The Kellner House

Who says ghosts have to be bad? Certainly not Peggy Kellner who co-exists quite amiably with a spectral housemate.

Peggy Kellner, who is wardrobe mistress of the Old Globe Theatre in San Diego, bought her vintage 1906 California bungalow (3342 Albatross, San Diego) in 1964. "This is it!" she decided instantly. "This is my house!"

"The place just kind of spoke to me, welcomed me somehow," she says in retrospect. "I didn't even bother to check the plumbing. I knew right away that for better or worse this was going to be my home."

Of course, she admits, things *do* happen . . . eerie, strange, unexplainable things. Once Peggy came home late from the theater determined to begin work on the costumes for an upcoming production of *Macbeth*. "I layed out the fabric and pattern on the dining room table," she recalls today. "As I snipped away, a tear drop crystal from the chandelier above fell on the material. Both the ornament and the main stem to which it had been fastened were intact. The crystal had somehow *unhooked itself.*

"I've got lots to do," Peggy reminded herself. She was not about to give up. The costumes were due the next day. She went on with her cutting. But when the same phenomenon occurred three more times and the ornate chandelier began to swing vigorously while everything else in the room remained stationary, Peggy decided the time had come to abandon her project.

"That was it," she recalls matter-of-factly. "I laid down my scissors and went to bed leaving the ghost to do her thing."

"Why do I think it's a female? Because a friend actually saw her," Peggy explains.

One day Pat Collins, then the Globe Theatre bookkeeper, was visiting. Peggy was in the kitchen brewing a pot of tea while Pat spoke to her through the open door. As Pat discussed finances, she idly ran her hands across the strings of an old harp. Suddenly a woman's voice said, *"Don't do that, just go sit down."*

Assuming that the voice was Peggy's but not taking the command seriously, she continued to pluck the strings of the harp. The words were repeated. Then before her astonished eyes there appeared an apparition of a woman in a long, white gown. Pat Collins was so startled that she ran from the house without even pausing to pick up her purse.

Peggy theorizes that her spectral roommate may be Victoria Pedrorena Magee, a tragic heroine of the pioneer days. Victoria, a California belle, eloped with a young doctor serving with the American occupation forces shortly after the acquisition of the new state. Her parents, detesting all Gringos, kidnapped Victoria and had the marriage annulled. A few years later, believing her beloved husband to be dead, Victoria attempted to escape the domination of her family by marrying yet another Yankee—Lt. Henry Magee.

The choice was an unfortunate one. McGee was a brawling braggart who dissipated much of his wife's fortune on liquor and fandango girls. In an effort to retain some independence, Victoria petitioned the state for the right to do business in her own name and was one of the very first California women to be accorded the concession. She salvaged the remainder of her inheritance, taught school and used her meager salary to purchase additional land. But, though proud, resourceful and spirited, Victoria was a victim of her time. For her, anatomy *was* destiny. She died at forty-four, her health ruined by numerous pregnancies.

Victoria's youngest daughter gave birth to a son, Cliff May—later to become a famous architect—in the charming bungalow where Peggy now lives.

Though Victoria Pedrorena Magee never lived in the house, Peggy believes that her spirit may be drawn to the place. "One thing is certain—this is a ghost who likes women," she says. "I feel very comfortable with her, but when men stay in the house alone—that's when the scary stuff starts happening."

She cites the experience of Phil Mathews, an Orange County psychotherapist who was staying in the house during her absence. It seems that Mathews was awakened from a sound sleep by a resounding crash. Running into the livingroom he was confronted by an eighty pound statue of three rococo cherubs which had pitched forward from a position on a buffet table causing a deep groove in the polished oak surface of the dining table some three feet away.

Frantically Mathews telephoned nearby friends, Judy and George Miller, urging them to come right away. As soon as the Millers arrived a painting of a madonna on the livingroom wall began to shake back and forth. That was the last time that Mathews ever stayed alone in the house.

"I think Victoria—or whoever it is—has her own ideas about how things should be arranged," Peggy says. "One evening I came home and lay down on the couch. It had been a long day and I was tired. I guess I fell asleep, but was suddenly startled awake by a loud crash. A picture had fallen from the wall. When I examined the wall I found that the nail that had held it was still sticking straight out of the wall as securely fastened as the day it was nailed. But that wasn't all. Not only had the picture somehow detached itself, but—instead of falling face down on the floor as one would expect—it was stacked neatly against the wall *facing inward.*"

Peggy did not replace the painting. "I assumed that the ghost just didn't care for it," she explains. "It seems that she has her own ideas about a lot of things. Could be my lackadaisical housekeeping displeases her. One Christmas season was particularly hectic for me. I didn't think I'd ever get caught up with everything that had to be done. Finally it got to be January 20th and I still hadn't taken down my tree.

"On the morning of January 21, I came into the livingroom and found that all the ornaments had been removed and neatly placed in their boxes beside the tree.

"You might think that someone was playing a joke on me—but who? I live alone!"

But Peggy is not the only one to have been a party to the strange goings-on in her home. Pat Collins—at last persuaded to return to the house—was awakened one night by the scent of mimosa. Though it was a warm summer evening, the room was suddenly terribly cold.

Another evening Peggy invited five friends to a dinner party. Later that evening the guests began to play kabala, a kind of mystical monopoly game. "We were chanting together to raise our energy when suddenly the kitchen cabinets began to bang open and then close," Peggy says. "Again and again this happened until we folded up our board and called it quits. Poltergeists were more than we'd bargained for."

Judy Miller tells of a time when she was house sitting for Peggy. "Suddenly I heard heavy footsteps coming up the porch steps and walking along the lengthy wooden veranda. The dog began to bark and ran to the door. I followed him and looked out. There was no one there."

This is a common occurrence, Peggy says. "Sometimes it'll happen three times in one evening. I'll be quite close to the front door and will open it quickly anticipating a knock only to find the porch completely deserted. Yet the veranda is so large that there just wouldn't be time for anyone to run away without my seeing him. There's a long porch, several steps and then an even longer walkway to the street. Where could anyone disappear to? Everything is visible from the doorway.

"Sometimes the women who come here are a bit startled by what happens but they recover quickly enough. No man ever house sits a second time."

Peggy has never tried to contact her ghost by seance or Ouija board. "We've got a good understanding," she explains. "Why stir things up? Whether the ghost is really Victoria Pedrorena Magee or not, I guess we'll never know. I do think it's a woman though. She's independent. I'm independent. We get along very well."

Los Angeles Area

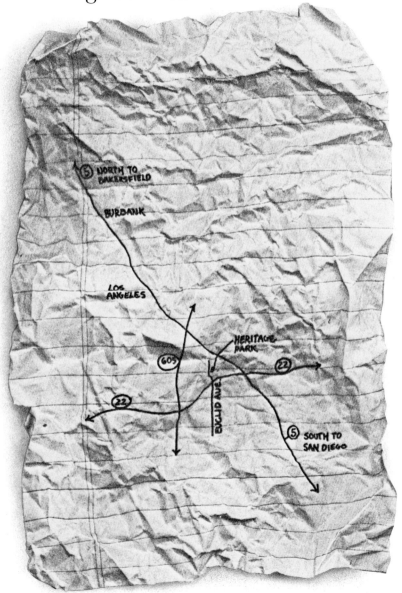

The Ghost Who Comes Back To Visit

On January 11, 1969 Yolanda Delgado Hosey died in a Los Angeles hospital under circumstances that were so medically suspect that a state investigation was later undertaken.

The twenty-two-year-old Yolanda was an exotic beauty. Two months pregnant, she would have celebrated her first year of marriage in just nine days.

That Yolanda's spirit has not accepted death became apparent when her invalid grandmother was awakened by an apparition—Yolanda. Because the elderly woman was herself terminally ill, the family had thought it best that she be spared the knowledge of her granddaughter's sudden and totally unexpected death.

The rest of the Delgado family was preparing to attend a rosary service when suddenly the old woman began to scream. "Yolanda's dead!" she confronted her relatives when they rushed to her bedside. "She was standing right here, right beside my bed in her wedding dress. I said, 'Wait, Yolanda, I'll come with you,' but she gave me a little wave of her fingers and turned away. I could see the train of her gown as she turned and then faded away."

Yolanda had been buried the night before—in her wedding gown. "She'd designed the gown herself and was so proud of it," Yolanda's mother, Carmen Delgado explains today. "The day she modeled it for me, she said, 'I love this dress so much—I want to be buried in it.' Who would have thought looking at the happy young girl that her wish would be granted in just one year."

The Delgados are a warm, closely knit family. Carmen explains, "We took our children everywhere with us when they were small and now that Yolanda's sisters, Rosie and Veronica, are married—a day doesn't pass that they don't call or come by."

Perhaps it's this loving atmosphere that continues to draw Yolanda. Salvador Delgado recalls a particularly memorable visit. It was December 21, 1969—his birthday. "I want to go with you," the grieving father pleaded as he stared at the apparition of his daughter.

Yolanda shook her head. "No, it's not your time."

"When is my time?" he asked.

Delgado says she seemed reluctant to reply, but when he persisted, Yolanda said at last, "1980."

When asked if Delgado feels apprehensive as the date approaches, he merely shrugs. "Why should I? Look at all the proof I've had. I'm certain that death is not the end."

Carmen Delgado has upon occasion heard the music of The Supremes, looked up—knowing that this was impossible—and seen Yolanda dancing to the music of her earthly favorites. Once she saw a vision of Yolanda poring over a wedding scrapbook. She seemed to be studying pictures taken at her sister Rosie's wedding, an event that she herself had participated in only a few weeks before her death. Beside her was another spirit—a young woman of about the same age.

"It's almost as though she brought a friend home," Carmen speculates. "I'd never seen the girl before but I'd recognize her now any place. She was very pretty with green eyes, blond hair worn in a pageboy and a very curvy body."

On that occasion Carmen spoke to her daughter, asking if she was happy. "Yolanda just shrugged. It was the other girl who answered me, saying, 'It's just that we get impatient sometimes.'"

Rosie also saw Yolanda with the same spirit friend. This time the spectral blond was reading a new issue of *Redbook*. "I was frightened," Rosie recalls today. It was the first time I'd seen her since her death. But she comforted me, calling me by name and telling me not to be afraid. I was pregnant then and very apprehensive because of Yolanda's death. She came to me often in those months, reassuring me that everything would be all right. She was with me in the hospital just before my daughter, Deana, was born. The next time I saw her was back at home bending over the baby's crib. Today Deana sometimes says, 'Mommy, there's someone in my room,' but so far she hasn't actually seen her aunt."

Perhaps the most dramatic event occurred about three years after Yolanda's death. Early one morning Carmen was awakened by a strange scraping or scratching sound coming from the livingroom. She immediately awakened her husband and they got up to investigate. Entering the livingroom, the couple was confronted by Yolanda sitting on the floor playing with a cat—a former pet, long since dead.

The Delgados described the images as faintly luminescent. "Don't worry Mommy and Daddy," Yolanda consoled them. Rising to her feet, she walked to within three feet of her startled parents. "I'll never leave you. I'm really lonely and miss all the family," she said and then slowly faded away.

Yolanda has been seen on many occasions by not only her parents and sisters, but assorted aunts, uncles, nieces, nephews as well as many outside the family circle. No one person seems responsible for triggering the phenomena, since the appearances have taken place in several different homes and with no one relative present on all occasions.

Not only are there apparitions, but poltergeist phenomena as well. Cold spots are felt, lights flash unaccountably. Plates suddenly break, glasses crack. Once the family cat was levitated to the ceiling and gently lowered to the floor—in full view of a half dozen persons.

In November 1971, Carmen Delgado—who is a member of the Southern California Society for Psychical Research—invited the group to her home. She informed them that the family had experienced poltergeist phenomena but did not go into detail about Yolanda's death or subsequent reappearance. Among those present was Dr. Ollie Backus, a practicing psychologist. A few days after the meeting, Dr. Backus conducted the final session of an ESP workshop which she had been teaching at St. Luke's Episcopal Church in Monrovia. "Most of the group," she reported later, "seemed to have something going that night. We were really hot on the ESP tests."

The following morning Dr. Backus went to her car and found the door hanging part way off its hinge. At a morning parapsychology class which she was also teaching at St. Luke's, Dr. Backus mentioned the unpleasant incident. A couple in the morning class, who had also attended the previous night, told her that their front door had been standing wide open when they returned home. Ordinarily, they explained, the door had a tendency to stick shut and was very difficult to open. During the course of the day Dr. Backus learned that two other individuals in the evening class had gone home to find their respective doors standing wide open.

At about the same time Carmen Delgado—unaware of all this activity—saw still another apparition. This was the spectre of a little girl who informed her, "Yolanda is in the house of the open door."

Nor was that the end of the open door policy. Yolanda, or what purports to be Yolanda, seems to make a habit of opening doors. One day Carmen and her sister-in-law approached the Delgado's front door in answer to a knock which they assumed was Carmen's brother. The doorknob turned and the door opened—but there was no one there.

Veronica, Yolanda's older sister, dreamed one night that Yolanda was showing her through a large house, then dismissed her, explaining, "We have to open the doors now."

Is the door business a rather mischievous means of attracting attention?

Hoping to better understand this strange set of circumstances, Carmen Delgado contacted the world famous medium, Peter Hurkos. Without being told the reason for her visit, Hurkos was able to establish clairvoyantly that she had lost a daughter. "She's with Maria now." (Maria was the grandmother first visited by Yolanda. The ailing woman had died two months later.)

"The doctor was at fault," Hurkos said. "He let her bleed to death—there is a witness." The accusation added to the mystery surrounding the young woman's death. Yolanda had been admitted to the hospital on December 12, 1968 complaining of severe abdominal pain. The doctor had at first refused to notify her husband who was serving in the army in Germany. "You're no different from any other pregnant woman. You must be strong," he'd chastised her. One month later she was dead without ever seeing her young bridegroom, Roy Hosey, again. Yolanda's death certificate gave the cause of death as pregnancy and vomiting.

During the course of the state investigation into the death, two nurses were fired and another disappeared. A doctor—an associate of Yolanda's physician—visited the Delgados and said with tears in his eyes, "Yolanda didn't have to die." The case was never resolved.

Does Yolanda come back in order to right a wrong? "We just don't know," Carmen sighs. "For a time the girls and I had a series of dreams that seemed to contain clues. The difficulty was how to read them and what to do about it. There was a nurse's name, for instance—a name that came to Rosie in a dream. We'd never heard it before. But sure enough when we checked, there had been a woman by that name employed at the hospital when Yolanda was there but she was gone and no one seemed to know where.

"Finding out what really happened doesn't seem so important to us any more. Nothing can bring our girl back to us as she was. The next best thing is knowing that she continues to exist somewhere and that one day we will all be together."

Heritage Park

Not only is Heritage Park (12174 Euclid Avenue, Garden Grove) haunted but possibly its young caretaker, Don Hayes, is as well.

One night, Don says, he was lying in bed wide awake when an apparition of a young man appeared before him. "You know who I am," the spectre said by way of introduction, then advised: "Don't take any bullshit."

"Unfortunately, I *don't* know who he is," Don admits, "but I do think a lot about his message."

Another strange incident occurred one evening when Don was rehearsing a play with the Scheherazade Players in an old barn at the rear of the park which has been converted into a theater. The seating capacity of the place is limited, the ambience intimate. "The audience is very close to the stage and we can see each individual quite clearly," Don explains. "While going over my lines I noticed an older man sitting in the front row. I assumed that he must be the father of a cast member but wondered why he was dressed in such old fashioned looking clothes. As soon as the scene was over, I started toward him to introduce myself—only to see him disappear before my eyes."

The Scheherazade Players—or possibly their barn—may have been responsible for still a different type of phenomena. While the group was performing *The Valkyrie*, a friend took a series of pictures. When the roll was developed they found what looks like bolts of white lightning superimposed over the original subjects. Many parapsychologists believe this type of phenomenon indicates the presence of spirits or spirit energy.

A highlight of the two acre Heritage Park is the Stanley House which was built in 1891 and has been retained in all its gingerbread elegance. Inside, two pictures continue to mystify a steady stream of tourists who come to view the old house which has been turned into a museum. First, there's the portrait of J. G. Chandler, whose serious face can occasionally break into an unexpected smile. Then, there's the more sinister visage of an unidentified man who appears to bleed at the throat. Studying the latter portrait carefully, one sees what appears to be tiny beads of blood forming just above the starched white collar spreading to a dark red line along the throat.

Recently a team from Psychic Science Investigators visited the house. Several felt climbing the stairs to the second floor that their progress was being impeded. Later, learning the background of the house, they discussed the former owner, Agnes Ware Stanley, and speculated as to whether they were not reliving a fragment of the pain and frustration which she must have felt as the years passed and she was no longer able to climb the stairs. (In the later years of Mrs. Stanley's long life the second floor was closed off entirely.)

Many visitors to the home have been puzzled by an unexpected noise, the sound of a baby crying in the upstairs nursery. Members of the PSI team heard it too. While resting their hands on the crib, some received impressions of an infant's death. It was later learned that Jennifer Null, the baby daughter of a former caretaker, had died in the room.

Yorba Family Cemetery

Some ghosts appear regularly on cue. They return again and again at the same time to the same spot—usually on an anniversary of life or death.

This is the case with the mysterious lady in pink who returns every two years to the Yorba family cemetery in Yorba Linda. The National Genealogical Society lists the small graveyard as the oldest in the state. Buried there are representatives of some of the grandest families in early California history. Existing headstones bear the proud names of Aguilar, Ames, Castillo, Celaya, Dominguez, Fuentes, Lugo, Murillo, Peralta, Reyes, Sepulveda, Vasquez and, of course, many Yorbas.

But there are others buried in the remote little cemetery, souls whose families were too poor to convey their feelings on costly tombstones. Many of these were buried under cover of darkness by relatives unable to pay the small burial fee.

Bernardo Yorba, a Spanish don, came to what is now Orange County in 1835 with a 13,000-acre land grant from Governor Jose Figueroa. Now only a historical landmark plaque attests that a gracious hacienda once dominated the area.

In 1858 Yorba set aside a secluded spot as a burial ground for family and friends. People say the evanescent pink lady is one of his daughters. Every two years her apparition is seen walking among the graves. Frequently she pauses to kneel before a particular tomb. Most of the markers are illegible now, but it's believed that she mourns at the graves of her mother and children.

No one can explain why this spectral visitation occurs always on June 15 on every second year, yet over the years scores of people have observed the phenomenon.

Unused since 1939, the tiny graveyard is all but forgotten. The setting is tranquil, the stillness broken only by the soft rustling of pepper-tree leaves. But the serenity was broken on the night of June 15, 1976 when some three hundred hopeful ghost watchers assembled to catch a glimpse of the pink lady.

Among them were PSI members. Security officers patroled the area carrying walkie talkies that suddenly refused to work. Flashlights, too, unaccountably failed. Suddenly the full moon was obscured by clouds—pink clouds.

Chris Metzner, a PSI leader, suddenly spoke: *"Por favor espere, yo voy!"*

"I don't speak Spanish," she explains today. "Someone had to translate it for me. I was as surprised as anyone to learn I'd said, 'Please wait, I am coming.'" Chris and the other members of her group believe that the spirit of the pink lady was speaking through her.

If so, it was the only contact that anyone made that night. But there's always next year.

Elke Sommer-Joe Hyams House

It began prosaically enough with afternoon tea. Elke Sommer invited Edith Dahlfeld, a German journalist, to have tea with her by the pool of her Beverly Hills home. It was July 6, 1964.

Glancing up from the tea table, Mrs. Dahlfeld saw a man come from the dining area of the house and walk toward them. Wondering idly why they had not been introduced, she watched as he strode briskly around the pool. Mrs. Dahlfeld was to describe him later as a middle-aged gentleman dressed formally in a black suit, white shirt and tie. His hair was thinning at the top, she said, and he had a bulbous "potato" nose.

Mrs. Dahlfeld's attention was diverted by the general conversation and she turned away from the solitary figure. Glancing back a few seconds later she was surprised to see that he was gone. "What happened to that man?" she asked.

Elke shook her head in bewilderment. "What man?" She had seen nothing. *There were no other guests.*

From then on Elke Sommer and her husband, Joe Hyams, began to hear the sound of chairs being pushed back in the dining room as though guests were rising from some ghostly dinner party. After a few nights of this Hyams cut away all the branches which might have been rubbing against the dining room window. The sounds *didn't stop.*

In August Elke went to Yugoslavia to make a movie leaving her husband alone in the house—or so they thought.

The noises in the dining room continued. On three occasions a locked window seemingly unlocked itself in the night and was wide open in the morning. Twice Hyams heard the front door open and shut even though it was found to be bolted in the morning.

Before joining his wife in Yugoslavia, Hyams arranged to have a detective check the house periodically in their absence. The man reported finding doors and windows wide open, although nothing was missing. Once, while driving by the house at two-thirty in the morning,

he discovered all the lights on. Just as he pulled in the drive, they all went off. An electrician checked the fuse box and lines but could find nothing wrong.

When the couple returned it was to the same restless dining room chairs. Now Elke's dogs began to react as though to a presence that no one else saw. "They would suddenly start to bark while staring toward the entrance of the dining room," Hyams recalls. "The puppy often ran to a certain spot in the dining room and then trotted out exactly as if following at someone's heels."

In August of 1965 the couple closed the house again and went on a month's vacation. During this time Marvin Chandler, the pool maintenance man, was surprised to catch a glimpse through the terrace windows of a man walking through the dining room. Chandler noted that the man's hands were clasped behind his back. He was a tall, heavy-set, elderly man wearing dark trousers, a tie and white shirt.

Having previously been told that the owners were away and the house empty, the maintenance man went inside to investigate. "He just seemed to evaporate before my eyes," Chandler recalls.

The apparition next appeared to John Sherlock, a writer who was staying alone in the house during the couple's absence. He reported seeing a man of about fifty dressed in dark slacks and a white shirt with a necktie but no jacket, standing in the family room which adjoins the dining room. "I have never had such a feeling of menace," Sherlock said later. "I couldn't get out fast enough." Although it was well past midnight, Sherlock dressed quickly and departed—spending the rest of the night in a motel.

The last witness was a real estate broker who was spending the night in the guest room. Once again the family was away and the witness was alone in the house. The apparition later described by the realtor was a middle-aged man who seemed to be searching for something. The ghost was seen in both the livingroom and the guest room.

On this occasion he was reported wearing dark slacks and a T-shirt.

Convinced that something thoroughly unpleasant was going on, the couple called in the American Society for Psychical Research. Dr. Thelma Moss of the Neuropsychiatric Institute, UCLA, organized a special group of investigators—mediums and researchers from the A.S.P.R.—to survey the house under controlled conditions.

Dr. Moss began by interviewing the witnesses. On the basis of their data, four measuring devices were devised. These included checklists of physical activities, descriptive adjectives, and qualities relating to the ghost, and a location chart of the house and grounds.

The witnesses were first asked to score the checklists. Then a number of psychics were invited to tour the house independently of one another. Afterward they were to indicate on the checklist their impressions of the ghost, his appearance and activities. Finally a control group of nonsensitives was asked to fill out the same forms *as if* they had seen a ghost in a house having such a floor plan.

The method outlined by Dr. Moss in the October 1968 issue of the American Society of Psychical Research began with the assignment of a draftsman to visit the house and make a rough sketch of the floor plan on its two levels, as well as a plan of the back garden and swimming pool area. The witnesses, the psychics and the non-psychic control group, were all asked to indicate on copies of the plan those areas where they felt the ghost had been seen or which they felt it had frequently occupied.

The "personality" of the ghost was defined by means of a checklist. Witnesses and subjects were asked to circle appropriate adjectives and to cross out adjectives opposite to the personality being described.

A list of forty active verbs was prepared describing various types of activities (musing, pacing, helping, laughing, floating, crying, dancing, eating, attacking, singing, etc.). Witnesses and subjects were asked to circle those activities which most accurately described what the ghost seemed to be doing and to cross out activities opposite to what the ghost appeared to be doing.

To establish the personal appearance of the ghost, another list was compiled. Here the items which the witnesses had mentioned were disguised by use of a multiple choice technique with many false items.

The experimental group included eight psychics who had worked before with the Southern California branch of the A.S.P.R. The control group comprised eight members of the society who did not believe that they could sense the presence of a ghost. The latter agreed to perform the same tasks as the experimental group.

In order to avoid any contamination of information, it was considered vital that the investigators who had interviewed the witnesses should not work with the eight psychics who comprised the experimental group and also that no investigator who knew one psychic's impressions would work with another psychic.

There were eight co-workers, one for each psychic. After driving the psychic to the house and being admitted by a servant, the co-worker remained in the livingroom while the psychic wandered as she or he pleased through all the rooms of the house as well as around the garden and pool area.

Each psychic was given a plan of the house and grounds and asked to indicate on it those places where he felt the ghost had been—or might be at the time of the visit.

Once the psychics had completed their tours and filled out their descriptive forms, the eight volunteer subjects comprising the control group met at the office of the Psychical Society. They were then instructed to fill out the location charts and checklists *as if* they had been taken to a house reputed to be haunted by a male ghost. All the subjects complied and their data was used in the statistical analysis.

The similarities found among the reports of the psychics and the differences discovered among the control groups were startling. None of the guesses made by the control group were in agreement when their checklists were tabulated and only one of them achieved even marginal similarity with the account of a witness. By contrast, *the psychics were very similar in their perception.* A consistent pattern emerged among them that was statistically significant: a composite ghost who appeared to be over thirty-five, tall and of medium to heavy build.

Maxine Bell, after touring the house, returned to the dining room where she described a sloppy looking spectre in his fifties. "I think he's a doctor," she said. "He died of a heart attack and is determined to stay in the house."

The next day another psychic, Brenda Crenshaw, entered the dining room and said, "I see a man, above average height, about fifty-eight, a doctor who died of a chest or heart condition outside the country."

Joe Hyams was reminded of a doctor with whom he'd been writing a book who had died suddenly while the work was still in progress.

Hyams then questioned the previous owners of the house. "I never saw anything unusual," the woman said, thinking back over her eighteen month tenancy. "But I heard strange sounds frequently." She told of an evening when her husband was out of town. Awakened from a sound sleep by the sound of footsteps in the dining room, she telephoned a friend and asked if she might go to stay with her. Locking herself in the upstairs bedroom, she called a taxi. A short while later the cab arrived and stopped in the driveway by the front door.

"I waited for the driver to ring the bell, but he didn't. Finally I shouted to him from the bedroom window. When he answered I ran down the stairs and into the cab. When I asked why he hadn't rung the bell, he replied that he'd seen a man standing by the door and assumed that he was the fare. The man vanished when I called out."

The following year Elke Sommer and Joe Hyams attempted to rent their home for the summer while they traveled in Europe. Mrs. Red Buttons, when brought to the house by a realtor, refused to enter. "It has an evil aura," she said, adding that she'd never felt that way about a house before.

Finally Mr. and Mrs. Harry Kanter rented the house. To celebrate the uneventfulness of their three month sojourn, the Kanters gave a "Good-bye Ghost Party." Sheet-clad guests had a pleasant—if uneventful time—until eleven-thirty when every light in the place went out. Suddenly a terrific crash was heard in the dining room. A wrought iron candelabra had crashed to the floor. It should be noted that there was no master switch to enable a practical joker to turn off all the lights simultaneously.

Elke Sommer and Joe Hyams moved back but the nocturnal activity within the house proved too much for them. They decided to move and began looking at houses. At last a selection was made. On March 12, 1967, the couple sat up late watching television—an old movie, *The Haunting.*

"I wonder what the ghost thinks about our moving," Hyams mused aloud. "If he has any opinion, he'd better express it pretty soon."

A few hours later Elke was awakened by the sound of pounding on their bedroom door. As Hyams opened the door he heard muffled laughter. The hallway was filled with black smoke. The couple escaped by leaping from their second-story bedroom window.

Hyams thought ruefully of a prediction made by Jacqueline Eastlund a few months before. "I see your dining room in flames next year. Be careful." At the time he'd considered raising his insurance and regretted not doing so later.

Lotte von Strahl returned to the house at Hyams' invitation. "The spirits have all been driven out by the fire," she assured him. The house could be rebuilt, it would be safe now.

Elke and Joe considered. The ghostly knocking had saved them from being burned alive. Perhaps it was a warning: *get out.*

And that's exactly what they did.

Central California

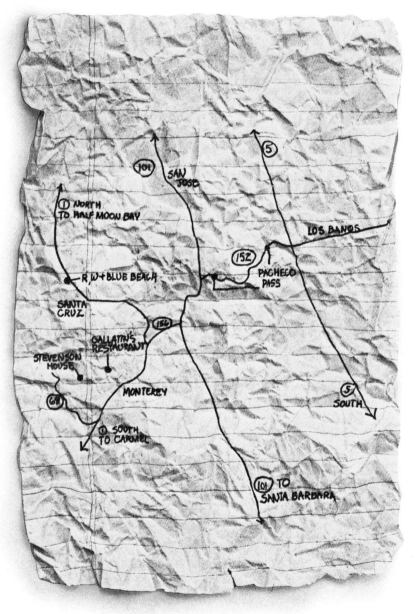

The Stevenson House

"Who is that woman in black?" the tourists sometimes ask, pausing in the doorway of the charming nursery.

Barbara Burdick, curator of the Stevenson House, a museum in the Monterey State Park, is at a loss to answer the question. The "who" remains a mystery. The "what" is for certain.

The woman in black is a ghost.

Legends are legion concerning the former boarding house now named for its most illustrious lodger, Robert Louis Stevenson. Many speculate that the "lady in black" is actually Fanny Osbourne—the alluring woman Stevenson came all the way from Scotland to woo and subsequently married.

But most—including Barbara Burdick—believe the ghost is Manuela Girardin, owner of the house during Stevenson's stay. They think the spirit of Manuela is in fact reliving the last tragic weeks of her life.

During the summer of 1879, Mrs. Girardin lost her husband, Juan, in a typhoid epidemic. Then in early December her two grandchildren fell ill of the same disease. Manuela worked desperately to save the children, tending them literally night and day. Then the devoted grandmother caught the fever from her young patients. She died on December 21st, never knowing that her grandchildren had recovered largely through her own efforts.

Over the years a variety of phenomena have been observed, almost invariably during the first three weeks of December. "People from out of state who know nothing of the legend will see all kinds of things," the curator says. "A rocking chair in the nursery will suddenly begin to rock of its own accord, or they'll smell carbolic acid—often a sickroom disinfectant.

"Each year an apparition is seen. 'Isn't it nice that the housekeeper is in costume just like you?' someone will say, pointing at what would appear to be a blank wall. Perhaps I wouldn't believe—not all the park employees do—if I hadn't seen her myself."

Late one foggy afternoon when Barbara Burdick was preparing to lock up, she noticed a woman in black gazing intently down at the children's bed. "She was oddly dressed in a long gown with a high lace collar, but aside from that looked as 'lively' as anyone," she recalls.

"Despite the stories, it never occurred to me that she wasn't just another tourist. When I explained that it was closing time, she nodded understandingly.

"I turned to leave and then looked back, wondering just how she had managed to get inside the barred room. The nursery was empty."

Haunted nursery
Photo by C.J. Marrow

Gallatin's Restaurant

Can love transcend the grave?

Consider the plight of Jehanne Powers, owner of Monterey's world famous restaurant, Gallatin's. The widow of Gallatin Powers who founded the place, she has bravely continued its management.

The award-winning restaurant is located at 500 Hartnell Street, in a grand mansion, circa 1838. Historically known as the Stokes Adobe, the building was once the residence of James Stokes, first American mayor of Monterey. Today it's an elegantly furnished dining house filled with valuable antiques.

The polished silver candelabra and exquisitely cut glass chandelier recall a time when Monterey was the Spanish capital of California. Surely many of the appointments were in the house during the exciting days when Monterey was menaced by the dreaded pirate Hippolyte de Bouchard. Others date from the tempestuous era when the capital was besieged by American forces. Could it be an energy implant, some psychic remnant of bygone terror that continues to "haunt" the restaurant today?

Kara Caswell, a partner of Jehanne's feels otherwise. "There are two kinds of things happening," she explains. "One kind involves ghosts that people see, the other involves things that happen. Maybe the ghost causes the happenings—they definitely appear to be directed by some kind of intelligence.

"Why am I so sure? Because most of the time the victims seem to be chosen for a reason. We'd discover that a certain employee hadn't been quite honest. Before we could fire him, he'd quit. The stories were always the same. 'Something' seemed to be shaking him, pushing him down the stairs, or he'd hear footsteps following him about the place late at night when he knew he was all alone. It seemed like a force was literally trying to shake these people up, telling them to shape up or get out—and that's exactly what happened.

"Once we had a bartender who was cranky. He could fix drinks well enough but the customers just didn't like him. It's hard to fire someone on the basis of personality alone but that seemed the only course to take. We didn't have to worry for long. He kept complaining about glasses falling off the bar. We didn't pay much attention and then one night I heard him yell. Rushing into the banquet room, I saw that the whole back bar—a massive mahogany thing—had begun to move. I thought for a minute that we were having an earthquake, but everything else was still. Not so much as a single prism of crystal from the chandelier was moving. That was the last we saw of the bartender. He left immediately."

Jehanne Powers believes that something has been trying to attract her attention as well. One night she and Kara closed the empty restaurant at 3 a.m. only to have the Muzak turn itself on full force as they reached the parking lot.

Many windows have opened by themselves and upon occasion every light in the place has turned on by itself even though there is no master switch. "One night the police called to report a light inside the restaurant," Jehanne recalls. "I remembered turning off every light myself. They wanted me to bring the key over so they wouldn't have to break in. I drove over and found the restaurant surrounded by police. One man took the key and went in. As he entered, he heard steps go up the stairs, cross the banquet room and go into a small room off to the side. The upstairs was quite dark but he could see the open door. 'Come out with your hands up!' he demanded. Instead, the door slammed shut knocking the gun right out of his hand.

"Finally, joined by reinforcements, he tore open the door. The tiny room—which has no window or exit—was completely empty. The police really don't like to come here any more and I don't blame them. Chasing ghosts does seem above and beyond the call of duty."

One evening Kara's young son, Charles, was polishing silver in the banquet room when he was startled by the sound of someone crying. Looking up, he saw the figure of a young woman in a long white dress. "I'm so sad," she said, wringing her hands.

Jehanne believes this to be the ghost of Evangeline Estrada whose sweetheart, Juan Escaba, was killed in the brief war for statehood.

"It's easy to imagine that the grieving girl might remain at the scene of her romance, waiting endlessly for her love to return," Jehanne speculates. "I feel sorry for her, but she doesn't frighten me. There are other entities that seem more ominous."

Again and again diners will ask about the lady in black. "Are you having a costume party upstairs?" one guest inquired recently. He explained that he'd glimpsed an older woman in a long black gown ascending the stairs. There was no costume party.

Another man felt a gown sweep the back of his chair. Turning to see if there was room for her to pass, he looked directly into the face of an older woman who seemed to melt into nothingness as she reached the stairway.

"I believe they're seeing the ghost of Hattie Gragg, a very strong-willed woman who lived in the house before my husband bought it," Jehanne says. "She was the last of a very proud family that had fallen into hard times. It was a tragedy for her heirs to have to sell the house but it had been mortgaged to the hilt. I think she bitterly resents strangers—restaurant guests—in her home."

Hattie Gragg's animosity toward the restaurant—and possibly herself—is only one problem facing Jehanne Powers. "I think my husband is in the restaurant too," she ventures. "Ours was a very close, extremely loving relationship. I think he wants me with him on the other side."

These fears have weighed heavily on Jehanne whose health has not been good. In an effort to find some answers, she called Sylvia and Dal Brown of the Nirvana Foundation.

The foundation is a psychic research organization; the Browns, gifted mediums, are its founders.

Without knowing any of the background of the restaurant, Sylvia walked about gathering impressions. At last she came to rest in the upstairs banquet hall, the scene of much of the phenomena.

"Gallatin is a family name but not the original one connected with this house," she said. "There has been much elegance here always. Many dignitaries have been entertained in this building when it was a residence. This lavish period seems to have reached its peak about seventy years ago. There is a woman—very prominant during that era—who refuses to leave the house. I hear her saying, 'This is mine.' But her feeling of hostility is mellowing. She no longer resents you. Her hostile vibrations may have caused your illness, but that should change now. She does not want you to die."

Sylvia continued, "There's a man here too, a very tall, large boned man. He has a lopsided grin."

"Yes—yes," Jehanne interrupted. "That's my husband. He was a very big man, 6'3", and he had a crooked grin. Does he realize that I must live out my life?"

Sylvia nodded. "Yes, he just wants to be near you. Some associates and employees have taken advantage of you. He has protected you from them and will continue to do so.

"Your health will improve," Sylvia reassured her. "The negative influences are out of the way now. You can enjoy your business and even your ghosts."

The seance ended on a bright note. Here was a ghost story with a happy ending—an ending that seems only the beginning as Jehanne's once critical health continues to improve.

Pacheco Pass

On January 30, 1977 Sylvia and Dal Brown were returning from a short vacation at Palm Springs. It was 6:30 p.m. and they had just reached Pacheco Pass on Highway 152.

They were passing San Luis Dam when unaccountably their good humored banter ceased. Sylvia felt suddenly overcome with anxiety. A lifelong medium, she has had countless brushes with the supernatural, but nothing comparable to this wave of sheer panic.

She glanced at her husband. He seemed oblivious to the turmoil that had enveloped her so completely. "This is what hell must be," she thought and started to pray. But prayer only increased Sylvia's discomfort; she could recall nothing beyond "Our Father." It seemed now that hundreds of voices were assailing her consciousness, strident, angry voices without words. Sylvia felt that she had been plunged into an endless void of pain and terror which seemed to have no beginning and no end.

"Help me!" she gasped, clutching Dal's arm.

"What is it, honey, tell me." Later she learned that he had repeated the words again and again, finally shouting them when she failed to respond. Sylvia had never heard him answer.

Dal, unable to pull off the road, continued to drive. Her sense of terror increased as images began to appear. She saw a little girl in a covered wagon cowering with her fists pressed against her eyes while Indians raged around the wagon train. Her sense of hopelessness was overwhelming. Scenes from a series of battles followed involving Spaniards, Mexicans, American settlers—all seemed to pass before her eyes in brutal succession.

"Those visions seemed to possess me, reason was useless," she said later. "Finally, as we reached the restaurant Casa de Fruita, they began to subside, but an intense depression replaced them.

"In an effort to reach out, I talked endlessly of the experience to my family and associates at the Nirvana Foundation. They were inclined to write it off as a psychic impression—well, I've had those all my life. It was more than that, it had to be. Somewhere along the lonely stretch of highway known as Pacheco Pass lurked something very real, very negative and very dangerous."

The intensity of Sylvia's impressions led her to believe that others must have shared the same experience. The flood of stories that followed her lectures confirmed this suspicion. The following are quotations taken from affidavits filed with the foundation:

"In many years of going over Pacheco Pass there has always been a deep feeling of desperate anticipation that something was going to happen to me. Also, I would have the most awful thoughts of death."

"I felt totally lost and I didn't care about anything, but there was a very strong sense of fear. I knew I shouldn't be scared. . .but I can't even explain how I felt other than to say lost, panicked, and very dizzy."

"While driving Pacheco Pass as a passenger on a very rainy night I became extremely frightened about going around the curves, although the driver was driving normally. I became really excited and asked the driver to stop for no apparent reason. We stopped and I became more excited; we finally drove on and the feeling subsided."

"Saw lights in the sky and had a horrible feeling of being trapped. My husband was asleep and I felt totally alone and alienated. I felt I couldn't get away."

To these, I must add my own experience. Driving the Pacheco Pass on a warm September evening in 1975, I experienced total, unexplained, unaccountable panic. Stranger yet, I couldn't get the idea out of my mind that I was being menaced by Indians. My fears began to dissipate after passing Casa de Fruita, but the depression remained for several days.

The most striking aspect of the phenomenon is the high degree of emotional involvement. All accounts refer to the anxiety experienced with no apparent cause. Sylvia Brown talks of a "nameless terror." Her intellectual control was blocked; not even simple prayers could be recalled. Terms that reappear in numerous accounts are "void," "alienated," "death," and "trapped."

Subsequent discussions with Sylvia uncovered another factor. A distortion of the local time structure seems to occur. She reports losing an hour while driving through the area. Two other persons experienced a time distortion. Their account reads:

"When we got to Fresno (from San Jose) and checked the time, we found that we had made the trip forty-five minutes faster than we ever had before. On the way back we lost one hour." An interesting point to note is that the experience occurred on January 30, 1977—the same day as Sylvia's encounter.

Sylvia believes the phenomenon is caused by an energy implant. This she surmises is a collection of highly emotional experiences that have occurred in the area. Over the years the energy from intense emotions has collected and become self sustaining. This energy, if sufficiently strong, causes a warp in the psycho-emotional structure of space-time. The warp acts like a gravitational field, pulling other waves of emotion.

The whirling boundary can be crossed; but, once inside, the rational mind may be totally overwhelmed by negative energy. Nothing is connected to time: it is all happening now—an eternal play. The foundation of one's reality slips away leaving only a sense of utter futility.

What could have caused such an implant? The Pacheco Pass area has a history of battles involving Indians, Spaniards, Mexicans and American settlers, many robberies by notorious highwaymen and a number of public hangings. Violence continues to this day in the form of numerous automobile accidents.

What obsession leads a driver to speed on a mountain highway? Could it be a compulsion to get out of there as quickly as possible? California Highway Patrol officers interviewed blamed "emotions" for many of the accidents and referred to survivors as "paranoid." A surprising number became involved in violent quarrels. An attempt to cut off or block another car may trigger a kind of war. Bumper tag may erupt into a violent fist fight—or a fatal accident.

The CHP says this irrational behavior occurs frequently on the pass. One patrolman remarked, "They're all trying to die quick up there. They're all crazy."

Suicide seems to be another not infrequent cause of death on the pass. People appear to run off the edge of the road for no apparent reason. A CHP lieutenant said, "I know people who won't drive through Pacheco Pass because they're scared to death of it."

With very good reason, it would seem.

Red, White and Blue Beach

A woman with a reputation for ghost chasing can expect to be asked anything. But most frequently, it's "Have you ever seen one?"

The answer is "no." I haven't seen ghosts, but I've surely felt their presence. One even accosted me at the nude beach in Santa Cruz.

It was the scariest night of my whole life.

It all began on another, far pleasanter evening. At a crowded Tahoe restaurant, a friend and I shared a table with another couple, Bill and Vivian Marraccino. The usual get-acquainted question, "What do you do?" led to surprises for everyone.

"Have I ever got a ghost for you!" Bill exclaimed when I told him that I was a writer specializing in psychic phenomena.

"There's this haunted house down in Santa Cruz—all kinds of stuff happens there. Things fly around the room, lights go on and off . . ."

"Tell her about the ghost," Vivian broke in. "It's an old sailor who walks out the back door of the house and strolls about the camp ground. He looks so picturesque in his old rainslicker and cap that a new guy—Jim Hilburn, an engineer —tried to photograph him. Jim got quite close to what he thought was a flesh and blood, if a bit eccentric, man. Then as he focused his camera, the old sailor faded away."

"Then there's the window," Bill picked up the narrative, "the window that doesn't exist." He explained that they and other campers at the Red, White and Blue Beach have often observed a lighted window on the hill above the water. "It really surprised me the first time," he recalls. "I couldn't remember any buildings in that area. I thought it was just a barren hillside with nothing on it.

"The next day I discovered that it *was* just a barren hillside with nothing on it."

Of course I had to investigate this one for myself. A few days later I drove to Santa Cruz intending to interview Ralph and Kathy Edwards, the owners of the house and camp grounds. Even on a sunny day the place looks like a setting for a Gothic horror story. Coast Road winds its way through deserted stretches of hills and sea. On a weekday in November there was very little traffic.

The nudists can't complain of peeping toms here, I noted turning off the road at the red, white and blue mailbox. Nothing else marked the narrow offroad which could easily be missed by passing motorists.

The narrow road wound downward from the highway, twisting and turning around rolling, mound-like hills. As I approached the isolated farmhouse, I felt that I had stepped back in time a hundred years. If ever a house looked haunted, this one did. The tall, two-story structure was like some lonely sentinel, a mute survivor. Of what, I wondered: penetrating fog and sea gales certainly. But what else?

Ralph Edwards met me at the gate. He was a tall, rangy man with a taciturn manner. "I hear you have a ghost," I ventured.

"Better talk to my wife."

"You mean you never saw it?"

"I didn't say that." He turned back to his gardening.

Kathy Edwards proved the opposite of her laconic husband. She was full of stories—all of them frightening. "Things are relatively quiet now—those footsteps, they aren't much. They happen so often, Ralph wouldn't get any rest at night if he ran downstairs to check every time we heard them. And the doors slamming by themselves, that's nothing. They do it most every day. My perfume bottles dance around a lot and we hear the sound of crystal shattering but never find anything broken.

"But when the girls were living at home, that's when the house was really active. My daughters used to have a terrible time at night. Something seemed determined to shake them right out of their beds. Sometimes they'd make up beds on the floor thinking to get away from it, but there was no escape. Every time they'd pull up the covers something would yank them away. I remember Ronda was working as a medical secretary—a really demanding job that kept her very busy. Sometimes I'd hear her pleading with the bed to let her sleep.

"My son, Roger, didn't believe his sisters, so one night he slept in Ronda's bed. Nothing happened and he was soon asleep. Then in the middle of the night he awakened thinking it was an earthquake. The bed was shaking so violently that it seemed to leap right off the floor.

"Since the girls married and moved away, whatever it is seems to have shifted its attention to the first floor. People just won't stay over night in this house. Our last guest was several years ago. A young relative sleeping on the couch was awakened by a rooster crowing. He could see its outline perched on the arm of the couch at his feet. But when he turned on the light nothing was there."

The Edwardses have never kept chickens.

Kathy tells of a Navy picture of Ralph's which was hanging in the livingroom. One night it flew off the wall and sailed five feet before crashing to the ground with a force so great that some of the glass splinters are still imbedded in the wood. The nail that had secured the picture remains in the wall.

"If you think any of this is funny, don't laugh too loud," Kathy advised. "I told a visitor about our ghost once and he laughed at me. That skepticism didn't amuse whatever lives here one bit. Suddenly a drawer opened by itself and a baby shoe flew out and hit him on the side of the head. That stopped his laughing in a hurry."

On Thanksgiving Day of 1975, Kathy Edwards was just opening the refrigerator door when a large plant left its standard and flew toward her—a distance of some twelve feet. Her daughter prevented a serious injury by grasping the heavy pot in mid air. But the mess could not be avoided. The plant and dirt that had been in the pot crashed against Kathy and splattered the inside of the refrigerator. No fruit salad served at that holiday dinner!

Ronda was the target of another attack which occurred one evening with nine people present. A glass of wine sitting on the piano flew through the air and deliberately poured itself down the front of Ronda's decollete dress.

"We have our own theories about that one," Kathy says. "Perhaps the ghost was jealous. In life she may have been very flat chested—Ronda definitely is not."

One mystery that continues to plague Kathy is the window on the hill originally described by the Marraccinos. "I kept hearing about the window; the campers were always asking about it. Then one evening I had to deliver a telephone message to the beach. As I walked back, I looked up and saw this great cathedral-like window on the side of the hill. It was very clear and I could see someone walking back and forth behind it.

"Something seemed to draw me toward the window, yet at the same time I felt that if I went there I'd never come back. I forced myself to return to the house. The next day I tramped all over the hill looking for some sign of what it might be, but found nothing. I never saw it again."

A few weeks later I returned to the house accompanied by a research team that included a group of mediums. The psychics walked about the house and grounds noting their impressions. I was the only one in the party who knew anything of the background of the place and I had not discussed it with anyone.

Chuck Pelton was the first of the mediums to speak. "There's a lot of current in the house, a lot of energy. Lights go on and off here by themselves."

"That's for sure!" Edwards affirmed. "The campers are always asking about those blinking lights. They say, 'Don't you and Kathy ever go to bed?' Actually the lights go on by themselves long after we've turned everything off and gone to sleep."

Chuck continued, "I see an old man wearing a raincoat and hat. I feel dampness, rain, mist. I think he was a sea captain."

This, of course, was corroborated by Kathy, who added that she'd found an old rain slicker and cap hanging on a hook on the back porch when they'd moved into the house. "At least a dozen people a year tell me they've seen an old man in a raincoat. I wonder sometimes if it couldn't be the sea captain who built this house in 1857."

The talking stopped. We were aware of the sound of animals howling outside. It was dark now and nothing could be seen from the windows. Chuck Pelton and Nick Nocerino went outside to investigate.

Sylvia Brown, co-director of the Nirvana Foundation, began to speak, "You feel a heaviness in your chest at night, don't you Ralph?"

"Yes," he nodded.

She continued, "Things move around in this house. They seem to get lost, disappear for no apparent reason."

"They sure do," Kathy agreed. "The first year we lived here we were ready for the divorce court. I thought he'd taken things; he thought I had. Now I know that neither of us had. It was someone else, something else. Once I had a letter to deliver for one of the campers. It disappeared right out of my hand and appeared a day later in a laundry bag."

"I see an older man," Sylvia said. "He's wearing a long coat and walks about the grounds. In his life he killed an intruder. He doesn't like company even now. The people who lived here before were an angry, unhappy family. There was a lot of hatred, a lot of unresolved problems. I see unhappy young people . . .a beautiful girl . . . blood. There was a stabbing here. A baby died here, too. There were evil acts committed in the past."

Nick and Chuck had returned and I was very glad to see them. The atmosphere of the house had grown heavy, oppressive. I had a sense of danger, an emotion that I'd rarely experienced in the other houses investigated over the years. A dog was whining softly, cowering under a chair.

Nick Nocerino, a lifelong medium, sat down beside me. His words were anything but comforting. "There has been evil in this house—murder and incest. I see an angry man who dominated his children. They were virtual prisoners here."

Kathy recalled that the former owner, a woman in her nineties, was the last of a large family who had lived for decades in the isolated farmhouse. "The stories she told me of her life were sad," Kathy said. "Her father took all the children out of school and refused to allow their friends to visit. He made his children work long hours in his dairy and then, as his health failed, he made them wait on him hand and foot. She seemed very bitter."

Nick went on, "There has been smuggling here—people mostly. People were brought here and some of them never left. They are buried here. There was bootlegging too."

"Yes," Edwards agreed, "we found bottles of home-made whiskey and the remains of a still."

"A young girl came to visit about the turn of the century. Her name was Gwendolyn. She was murdered."

Kathy gasped. "A girl named Gwendolyn did disappear mysteriously while visiting her uncle, who owned the place. That was in the very early 1900s. No one ever heard from her again. But a couple of years ago Ralph and I decided to put in a barbecue pit and dug up a skeleton.

50

We thought it might be an old Indian burial ground and called in an expert from UC Santa Cruz. He said the bones were those of a woman buried seventy to eighty years ago."

The number of amazing "hits" says a good deal for mediumship, but did little to allay my fears. Directly across from where I sat in the livingroom was a window facing out onto the front yard. From time to time I saw streaks and blobs of light at the window. It's my imagination, I told myself.

I could live with that until Ethel Pelton who was sitting on the floor opposite me and directly under the window, spoke in a tight, choked voice. "I feel something terrible behind me. Something's going on outside, I know it is and I'm scared."

It really didn't help to have my skeptical friend, John Wilson, a Menlo Park attorney, confide that he too felt a sense of dread and oppression.

It was nearly midnight as the seance broke up. John and I walked out into the black night. A thick fog was creeping in from the sea. I felt certain that the evil presence menacing the house had attached itself to me. Sick with terror, I stood shivering in the damp sea air—uncertain whether to continue on in the dark or go back into the afflicted house.

John made the decision for me. "Come on, let's get out of this place," he said, grasping my arm and pulling me toward the car. Just as we got in a great dark bird appeared out of nowhere and hovered above us. As we slowly navigated the narrow dirt road to the highway, the ugly creature preceded us. It had a wingspan of some six feet. What was it, I wondered—an owl, an eagle? I recalled that the place had at one time been known as the Eagle Run Dairy. What a relief when this gruesome harbinger of doom finally faded away in the night.

But that was not the end of our troubles. A heavy wind seemed to come up out of nowhere as we crossed the Santa Cruz mountains, making it difficult to keep the car on the road. I began to see flashes of light like bolts of lightning and blobs of white energy. There seemed no doubt that some evil presence was pursuing us.

Some of that apprehension dissipated in the familiar atmosphere of my apartment. The streaks were gone, the blobs were gone, yet I could not rid myself of the feeling that I was not alone. Many times in the days that followed, I glanced up from my typewriter, certain that someone was looking over my shoulder.

Had I picked up a spectral hitchhiker? I recalled the story of "Lu," a woman who'd visited the farmhouse with her boyfriend, a long time friend of the Edwardses. Lu had felt so uncomfortable in the house that she'd left almost immediately. At home, she experienced a sense of possession. Again and again she heard the words, *unfinished* and *unburied.* She saw a vision of a man and large searing white spots.

Slowly as the days passed, the sense of being watched diminished. I was alone again—really alone—and very glad of it. It was all imagination, I decided, and was beginning to believe it. And then one evening Nick called.

It seemed that he and Chuck had photographed the house while outdoors investigating the howling sounds. "What did you get, werewolves?" I tried to sound flippant.

"No, just blobs and streaks of light," he answered, also trying to sound flippant.

The pictures had been taken in darkness and yet the house was clearly revealed. The upstairs window of a darkened bedroom was illuminated and above the livingroom—where the seance had taken place—were round blobs of light and sometimes lightning-like bolts.

Some nights I wonder what they're doing down at the nude beach—but so far, I haven't had nerve enough to go back and find out.

San Jose

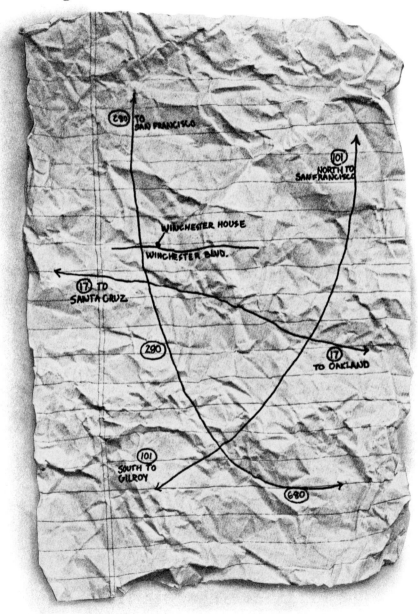

The Winchester Mystery House

Every night is Halloween at Sarah Winchester's house.

An aura of mystery and dark foreboding surround the awesome structure. The towering spires, minarets and coupolas stand dark and still, silhouetted against the sky. Inside there are trap doors, secret passageways and doors which open into the air.

The Gothic Victorian is a living monument to the dead. The legend of Sarah Winchester, who tried to shut off the grim realities of life and death with a carpenter's hammer, is everywhere.

The story of Sarah Winchester—surely the most enigmatic woman in the history of the West—is a fascinating one, as is the legend of the house itself. To the pioneers of the 19th century, the Winchester repeating rifle was "the gun that won the West." But to Sarah Pardee Winchester, heiress to the fortune of the Winchester Repeating Arms Co., the weapon was an instrument of doom and ultimate destruction for herself.

According to the story, the widow of the rifle manufacturer's only son was informed by a Boston medium that the spirits of those killed by Winchester rifles had placed a curse upon her. The medium advised Sarah that she might escape the curse by moving west and building a house. As long as the building continued, the vengeful spirits would be thwarted and Sarah would live.

The unhappy heiress obediently moved to California and purchased an eight-room farmhouse which she proceeded to remodel literally as the spirit moved her. The construction project, begun in 1884, was to occupy the next 38 years of her life and would ultimately employ hundreds of artisans working on a 'round the clock basis that included Sundays and holidays.

Design conferences took place in the seance room where Sarah retired each night. Her spectral consultants were capricious and insatiable, demanding room after room, balcony after balcony, chimney after chimney. The strange growth spread until it reached a distant barn,

Sarah Winchester in the late 1800's
Photo courtesy of the
Winchester Mystery House

flowed around and adhered to it like a tumor, and finally engulfed it. An observation tower shot up, only to be choked by later construction until nothing could be seen from it.

To the original eight rooms, hundreds were added, many of them quickly ripped out to make way for new ideas from Mrs. Winchester's nocturnal advisors. Today, one hundred and sixty rooms of this baffling labyrinth still stand, the survivors of an estimated seven hundred and fifty chambers interconnected—if one can use that term—by trick doors, self-intersecting balconies and dead-end stairways.

Literally miles of winding, twisting, bewildering corridors snake through the house while numerous secret passageways are concealed in the walls. Some end in closets, others in blank walls. The door from one was the rear wall of a walk-in icebox. The halls vary in width from two feet to regulation size and some ceilings are so low that an average size person must stoop to avoid bumping his head.

The explanation for all this is that the house was devised by ghosts for ghosts. If ghost stories are to be believed, spirits dearly love to vanish up chimneys. So Sarah obligingly provided them with not one but forty-seven of these escape hatches.

Dining in splendor with her secretary-companion, Mrs. Winchester frequently enjoyed the best vintage wines. One evening she went to the wine cellar—to which only she possessed the key—to locate a special bottle. To her horror, she discovered a black handprint on the wall. That night the spirits confided that it was the print of a demon's hand. Sarah took this as a warning against alcohol and had the cellar walled up so thoroughly that, to this day, the liquid treasures have never been found.

The seance room where Sarah received her instructions was off limits to other humans. Those entering the forbidden sanctuary after her death found a small blue room furnished with only a cabinet, armchair, table, paper and planchette board for automatic writing.

The capricious mistress of the manor indulged her whimsey by never sleeping in the same bedroom for two consecutive nights. In this way she hoped to confuse unwanted spirits, but it was her servants who were confused after the 1906 earthquake. Following the severe tremor it took the staff nearly an hour to finally locate their frightened mistress who had been trapped inside a room when the wall shifted, jamming the door.

Sarah believed the terrifying experience had been inflicted upon her as a punishment for her extravagance in constructing the front of the house. To placate the spirits, she ordered the front thirty rooms sealed off and never used. This included the grand ballroom which had been built at a cost of $9000 and a stained glass window costing $2000. The costly front door was used by only three people—Sarah Winchester and the two carpenters who installed it.

Despite all her efforts, death came to Sarah Winchester on September 5, 1922. Today one can still see half-driven nails where the carpenters stopped when word came that the eighty-five year old recluse had died quietly in her sleep.

Of her $21-million inheritance, the widow spent at least $5.5-million pre-inflation dollars to please her discarnate friends. Unless ghosts are unspeakable ingrates, Mrs. Winchester should have been well received on the other side.

But was that the end of the story? Hardly, to judge from the weird tales surrounding the house. Over the years a variety of psychic phenomena have been reported —chains rattling, whispers, footsteps—a Gothic thriller seemingly come to life.

In order to investigate these claims, the Nirvana Foundation obtained permission to spend a night in the house. There were five in our party: Dal and Sylvia Brown; Dick Schaskey, head of the photography department at San Jose State University; Ann Fockelmann, a research associate at the foundation; and I.

Throughout the long night Sylvia, Ann and I saw moving lights for which we could not account. All of us felt sudden gusts of icy wind and cold spots. While sitting in Mrs. Winchester's bedroom, Sylvia and I saw great balls of red light that seemed to explode before us.

As the rest of us sat on the floor of the bedroom clutching our clipboards and cameras, Sylvia saw a couple who, she claimed, watched us intently from across the room.

During the thirty-eight years that Sarah Winchester resided in the "mystery house," her servants and other employees remained fiercely loyal, defending her every eccentricity. They described her as strong-minded and firm, but always fair and kind. Each was well paid and some were rewarded with lifetime pensions or real estate.

In death, it would appear that Mrs. Winchester received the same attention from her servants as when she was alive. "The man and woman that I see are dressed in clothing popular during the turn of the century," Sylvia explained. "They're caretakers, I think. Their attitude isn't really menacing but they are watching us very carefully. They don't seem to like strangers in their house."

As the night wore on the frightening sense of being observed did not diminish. We sat for about an hour watching a ghostly shadow play across the dark walls. Each of us tried to explain the spectral light show in earthly terms. Moonlight? There was no moon. Passing cars? The few windows faced onto a dark courtyard. There were no cars.

It was a very long night.

A daylight bustle had settled over the place as we wearily carried out our equipment the next morning. Maintenance of so large a structure never stops. The sounds one hears during the day are anything but spectral. The carpenter's hammer echoes just as it did during the mansion's heyday.

So it would seem that Sarah Winchester does, indeed, live on as her home does—achieving her own kind of immortality.

San Francisco Bay Area

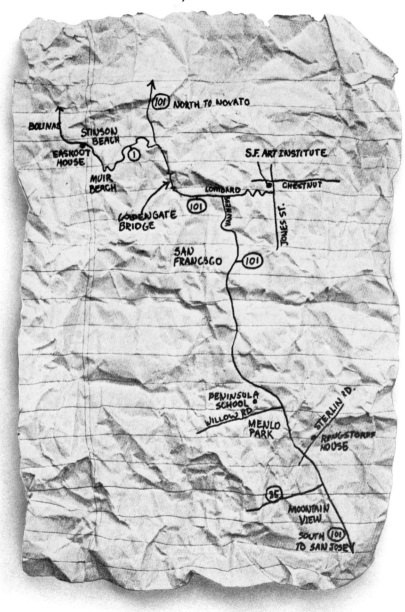

Atherton Mansion

Who rules the roost at the historic Atherton house? The domineering matriarch? The ineffectual son? The rebellious daughter-in-law? Or the mysterious cat lady?

Can the battle of the sexes transcend the grave?

Consider the cast of characters. First there is Dominga de Goni Atherton who built the house—now a historical landmark—in 1881. During the lifetime of her millionaire husband, Faxon Dean Atherton, she was condemned by convention to a subservient role. While Faxon spent most of his time tomcatting around San Francisco, she did the family homework—managing their country estate. (The town of Atherton evolved from these holdings.)

Immediately upon Faxon's death, Dominga bade a hasty farewell to surburbia and established permanent residence in the city. Construction of the impressive mansion at 1990 California was, in a sense, her declaration of independence.

Then there was Gertrude Atherton, Dominga's audacious daughter-in-law who shocked the haughty Athertons by writing racy novels. And finally there was George, who barely had the initiative to tie his own shoelaces.

During the 1880s, Dominga financed George in a series of financial ventures that invariably failed. Then one evening in 1887, the California Street house was the scene of a grand ball honoring visiting Chilean naval officers. "It was a brilliant affair, one for which the new house was admirably suited," Gertrude wrote in her memoirs.

"There were dowagers with acres of whitewashed flesh . . . bulging above corsets . . . hips as large as their bustles; girls in voluminous tulle, all looked me over disapprovingly."

That was because Gertrude had disdained the traditional ball gown, wearing instead a devastating creation of white cashmere which she described as "fitting every part of me like a glove."

Gertrude enjoyed the disapproval of the good ladies of San Francisco. But George did not enjoy *her* disapproval —Gertrude had called him a "mere male, nothing more"—

and at the height of the party, he impulsively accepted the Chilean guests' invitation to accompany them back home.

The following day when George showed signs of relenting, Gertrude outmaneuvered him. She was not about to allow a few Georgeless months to slip through her fingers. Cleverly she goaded, "If you have any pride you will stay here in San Francisco and make something of yourself."

He left.

Gertrude got even more freedom than she bargained for. After a few nights at sea, George died of a kidney attack. The captain decided that the San Francisco scion should be shipped home for burial. Hoping to preserve him, the resourceful Chileans placed the body in a barrel of rum and continued on to Tahiti where another captain agreed to take George back to San Francisco. According to legend, the family first learned of his demise when the cask was delivered to 1990 California, where an unsuspecting butler uncrated his pickled master.

"I had an uneasy feeling that George would haunt me if he could," Gertrude admitted. She didn't linger in the area, literally taking her inheritance and running.

The mansion had a quick succession of owners. Then, in 1923, Carrie Rousseau remodeled the place into separate apartments, selecting for herself the thirteenth unit—formerly the orchestra chamber of the grand ballroom. Sharing an adjoining apartment—once the banquet hall—were her fifty cats.

Carrie died in 1974 at ninety-three, attended by only her feline companions. Human tenants knew little of her but had plenty to say about the spectral inhabitants of the house. Singer Aurora Booth, when interviewed by *San Francisco Chronicle* reporter Kevin Wallace, described a rushing wind that roared through her tiny apartment. Jerrie Landewig, a dental assistant, complained of rapping on her bedroom door just as she was dropping off to sleep, and told of a former tenant who was frightened out of his tower apartment by filmy apparitions.

These witnesses, who have since moved from the house, were quite certain that George was the spirit causing the excitement. But at a seance held in July of 1976, medium Sylvia Brown picked up on three female spirits. "They just don't like men," she warned the two current owners—both men.

Unaware of the house's history, Sylvia began to pick up psychic impressions of the apparitions which appeared before her. "One keeps saying, 'This is *my* dwelling.' She seems awfully possessive," Sylvia said. "She's short, very buxom and highly volatile, a lot of energy there." (Dominga Atherton weighed two hundred pounds and was five feet tall. A native of Chile, she possessed a firey Latin disposition.)

The next apparition was described as an attractive blond with "very definite likes and dislikes, very independent for her time. She wanted to be liberated and was." (An apt description of Gertrude, if her own writings are to be believed.)

The third apparition, subordinate to the others, was identified as "Carrie."

Hot and cold running spirits made the evening memorable. Room temperatures changed frequently and drastically, keeping the eleven of us who participated in the seance busy taking off and putting on our jackets and sweaters.

Photographs taken that night by Nick Nocerino reveal a series of spectral "blobs" that seem to float about the house. Tape recorders picked up a strange moaning sound that no one heard during the seance, but did *not* pick up the sound of a tinkling bell—the type used to summon servants—which was clearly heard by all.

"There *is* a male spirit here," Sylvia said at last, "but he's so pale and frail. There's nothing to fear from him. But bad vibes could come from female ghosts who want things done their way and won't tolerate much male interference."

Does feminism transcend the grave? Sylvia Brown believes that it does and suggests that the Atherton mansion would make a dandy women's resource center.

Haskell House

"Fire! . . . one . . . two." In the time it took to say those three words, California's most famous duel occurred, the Broderick-Terry affair.

U.S. Senator David C. Broderick had been a New York saloonkeeper and Tammany henchman before coming to gold-rush San Francisco, according to his own accounts, "sick and penniless." Before long he was literally coining money—taking gold dust and turning it into five and ten dollar gold pieces at a handsome profit.

With health and finances improved, Broderick studied history, literature and law and was admitted to the bar; then ran for the state senate and became its president. By 1851 he was in absolute control of San Francisco's political machinery—adored by some, detested by others. One historian described Broderick as "the rudest, roughest, most aggressive young man in the area." The young politician made either friends who would die for him or enemies who would make him die if possible.

State Supreme Court Justice David S. Terry was equally pugnacious. When the two met for their fateful duel, he had only recently been released after stabbing a Vigilante officer.

The two men were fiercely divided on the issue of slavery. Terry, a Southerner steeped in the traditions of plantation society, was determined that California become a slave state. Broderick was equally determined that it would not.

Of all the free states, California had the most stringent laws against blacks. Shortly after achieving statehood, the California legislature enacted a law that virtually made slaves of freed blacks. Under the law a black man or woman could be brought before a magistrate, and claimed as a fugitive. Since the seized individual was not permitted to testify, the judge had no alternative but to issue a certificate of ownership to the claimant.

Anyone who gave assistance to a fugitive was liable to a fine of five hundred dollars or imprisonment for two months. Slaves who had been brought to California by their masters before statehood, and had since been freed by a constitutional prohibition of slavery, were held to be fugitives and were liable to arrest although they may have been free for several years. Though it was obvious that the intention was as much to kidnap free blacks as it was to apprehend fugitives, the law was re-enacted year after year.

Outspoken criticism of the practice did little to endear Broderick to the many influential Southerners in government—Terry among them.

There was an angry exchange of words and then a challenge. The two would settle their dispute with a duel. Broderick spent the night prior to the fateful meeting with a close friend, Leonides K. Haskell at his charming bayside cottage near Black Point. It was clear to Haskell that his friend was in no condition to risk his life. He had just completed an exhausting political campaign in which his health had been a problem. The night before the duel he lay on the floor until the early hours of the morning drinking coffee and talking. Haskell said later that Broderick was "fey—all night," that is, a man deeply disturbed.

But in the morning Broderick smiled reassuringly as they climbed into the carriage that would take them to the appointed place, a farm near Lake Merced just over the San Mateo County line.

The behavior of the two parties was in sharp contrast as they met in the early morning sunlight. While Terry's seconds were cool and assured, Broderick's men were uncertain and inexperienced. Haskell partially removed Broderick's cravat and then, overcome with emotion, walked away and stood for a moment wringing his hands in anguish. Sadly he returned at last to finish his task.

Broderick's own confidence had returned and he looked out at the crowd of some eighty spectators who'd gathered, nodding to some.

A toss of a coin determined position and weapons to be used. Terry won and his pistols were produced and loaded. They were of Belgian make, eight-inch barrels

which used Derringer-size balls and hair triggers. He had practiced often with them.

The gunsmith who loaded Broderick's pistol warned that the trigger was set too finely, it could be set off merely by a jerk or jar. His objections went unheeded. Broderick's hands changed position repeatedly as he tried to get the feel of the weapon.

The seconds stood back, leaving the principals to face one another from an ominous distance of twenty paces.

"Gentlemen, are you ready?"

"Yes," Terry replied promptly. Broderick hesitated an instant then nodded.

Both men shot between the words "fire" and "two." Broderick's bullet spent itself in the ground about nine feet in front of him. The weapon had fired as he raised it. Terry's bullet struck the senator in the chest, staggering him. For a moment Broderick stood erect, trying to brace himself and then fell backward onto the grass.

For a second the shots echoed in the still morning air. Then a half strangled cry came from the crowd, "That's murder, by God!" A surgeon hurried forward to stem the crimson flow that poured from the wound, while Terry remained erect, still in the classic stance of the duelist.

A wagon was brought and the senator was gently lifted and placed on a mattress within it. The party set off for the Haskell home retracing the route they'd taken just an hour before. Upon arrival Broderick was carried to a second floor bedroom which overlooked the sea. Physicians tended him around the clock. At first their reports were optimistic, then they changed as his condition worsened.

Broderick's sorrowing friends gathered around the bed. For three days their hopes rose and fell. At times Broderick conversed in heavy whispers, his body racked with pain. "They have killed me because I was opposed to the extinction of slavery and a corrupt administration," he said at last. Shortly before midnight on September 16, 1857, Broderick lapsed into unconsciousness and at twenty minutes past nine the following morning he died.

But the duel, instead of turning California toward the South, had an opposite effect. In the hue and cry that arose over Broderick's death, the once powerful Southern faction heard its death knell. Broderick dead was a far more powerful man than Broderick living. A heretofore indifferent populace rallied round a martyr's grave. Perhaps Terry, in the thirty years before another man's bullet ended his life, had cause to ponder the paradoxical failure of a plan that succeeded.

But many think that death was not the end of the thirty-five-year-old senator. Surely Haskell must have felt the loss keenly. It was at his home that Broderick had first received Terry's challenge, and the two were together constantly until Broderick's death six days later.

Haskell remained in the house with its tragic memories until 1863 when the land was annexed by the military.

Over the years a succession of tenants have complained that the place is haunted. A man in a long black coat with a top hat has been seen many times pacing back and forth. Could this be Broderick reliving his anguish on the night before the duel? Many people have thought so.

Colonel Cecil Puckett, who lived in the house in 1975-77, tells of a presence in the kitchen. "I feel that something or someone follows me about the house at times," he says. "I even feel that it watches me in the shower."

Sylvia Brown, while investigating the house, saw clairvoyantly a whole mosaic of spirits. "Black people were hidden in the cellar," she says. "They were hidden for their own good, but many of them were frightened and unhappy, uncertain of the future."

Considering the state of San Francisco politics in the 1850s, this seems highly probable. Surely Haskell, an anti-slavery crony of Broderick's, would have aided fugitives even to the extent of hiding them in his home.

Those turbulent times have left their imprint on the pretty two-story house where many dramatic events must have taken place over the years.

Of course it's haunted.

San Francisco Art Institute

Can unfulfilled longings trigger a ghost into being?

A group of prominent psychics hold frustrated creativity to blame for a series of hauntings that have mystified faculty and students at the San Francisco Art Institute (800 Chestnut Street).

The Institute is a splendid example of the Spanish Colonial revival architecture popular during the 1920s. The walls are stripped concrete dyed a soft adobe ocre under red tile roofs. A bell tower rises above the patio in the manner of an early mission.

"There's something strange about the bell tower," students began to whisper almost immediately after the Institute opened its doors on January 15, 1927. But it was twenty years before anything *really* happened.

Artist Bill Morehouse is now chairman of the art department at Sonoma State College, but in 1947 he was a night watchman and student at the Institute. To reduce expenses, he decided to sleep in the tower.

He vividly recalls his first night there, even after thirty years. "It was around midnight and I had just gone to bed on the third level. I heard the doors opening and closing down below. I'd locked them myself, but I assumed that it was the janitor, so I didn't bother to investigate. I listened to the footsteps climbing to the first level, then to the second and finally to the third. The door knob turned and the door to my room opened and closed as though someone had entered. It was a large room and well lighted. Inside was a water tank, my bedroll and me. I saw no one but heard footsteps passing through the room, turning, then walking back to the door. The knob turned, the door opened and closed and the footsteps continued up to the observation platform."

That was Morehouse's first encounter with the Art Institute Ghost, but not his last. He tells of another night when he and five friends were partying in the tower. Their laughter came to a sudden halt at the sound of footsteps approaching. "The steps came up, up, up," he says, "just as they reached the landing, one of us yanked the door

65

open and yelled 'surprise!' We were the ones who were surprised—there was no one there. The steps continued on, going all the way to the top of the tower."

Wally Hedrick, long-time faculty member, said his most frightening brush with the ghost occurred one night when he was working after midnight. Suddenly, he heard all the tools go on downstairs in the sculpture studio. Hurrying down to investigate, he found no one.

Working as evening registrar during those days was Hayward King, now curator of Bolles Gallery. Like many others, Hayward also began to believe in the ghost. He remembers closing the school at 10 p.m. "There was no master switch then, so we would walk all around the Institute, turning off the lights as we went. Just before going out we'd turn and look back. Often we'd find that one or two lights were on again in the empty building. Of course, you could say that we'd missed those lights or there was a short in the electricity. You could say a lot of things . . ."

Once King and Hedrick closed the office together after all the lights had presumably been turned off. As they shut the front door, every light in the building turned on simultaneously.

Morehouse, Hedrick and King believed their ghost to be mischievous but essentially benevolent. The unexplained manifestations that livened their evenings became less and less frequent until the ghost was almost forgotten.

Then in 1968 it returned. This time its appearance was decidedly disturbing.

As a 1.7 million dollar enlargement program began, attention was once more focused on the tower, which was being renovated as a storage facility for the Institute's Art Bank Collection. It seems that a slumbering ghost was awakened.

Several students on the night maintenance shift were convinced that the ghost was not only an evil influence on their own lives but was holding up the construction project. Three of the night crew blamed the spirit for personal disasters that included a serious motorcycle accident, an attack of polio and a tragic family situation.

Another told of studying late at night in the library with his wife. "We heard the sound of chairs being broken behind us, but no one was there," he said. The building program was delayed for many months by a series of costly mistakes and near-fatal accidents.

In October 1976 a group of psychics gathered for a seance in the Institute tower. With them were several observers, myself included. Frustration was the emotion picked up by all the mediums. "So many artists with such grand designs that never got anywhere . . . so many trying to put their ideas on canvas . . . Many projects uncompleted."

San Jose medium Amy Chandler told of seeing a "lost graveyard," a fact later verified by the Institute historian. A cemetery adjacent to the Institute has been obliterated by early 20th Century construction.

A series of pictures taken that evening by Nick Nocerino revealed the tower room not as it was but as it had been—with a door and windows that no longer exist. Others taken by Chuck Pelton showed a strange displacement of people within the room—a kind of musical chairs effect. Seance participants were photographed in motion, some fading in and out entirely. In reality none of us moved from our chairs during the two-hour session.

What that means, only the ghost can explain.

67

Montandon Townhouse

"I lay a curse upon you and upon this house; I do not forget and I do not forgive; remember that!"

Can evil, angry words carry a power of their own? Is fact truly stranger than fiction?

Pat Montandon certainly has reason to think so. After reading her book, *The Intruders*, one finds it difficult to disagree.

During the 1960s the dazzling blond achieved recognition in San Francisco as hostess of a popular TV show. She gained national fame when listed by *Esquire Magazine* as one of the top hostesses in the country. The image, sustained by many flash bulbs and much newsprint, was "glamorous jet set queen." Here was a woman who seemingly had everything.

Unfortunately "everything" included a haunted house on Lombard Street.

It all began with a party, one more gala star-studded event in a glittering chain. This gathering—in keeping with the astrological renaissance of the late sixties—had a zodiac theme. An added attraction was a Tarot card reader.

The warm, festive mood turned to chill when the seer, piqued by an imagined slight, suddenly turned on Pat and snarled, "I lay a curse upon you . . ."

The words returned to haunt her in the years that followed, fearful years that found the golden butterfly ensnared in a web of dark malevolence. Her house was repeatedly vandalized and fire-ravaged. Her car was smashed several times, her career disrupted, her reputation threatened by ugly accusations, her romances blighted.

Locked windows within the house opened of their own accord. A biting chill defied the normally functioning heating system and totally destroyed the warm ambience of the luxury townhouse. Two close friends who shared the house committed suicide. Repeated threats on Pat's own life forced her to hire round-the-clock guards but they could not protect her from the evil atmosphere that seemed to pervade her very being.

"I don't believe that the Tarot reader caused these things," she emphasizes today. "But possibly something in that ugly incident triggered evil forces already hovering about me or about the house itself—once the scene of public hangings.

"Such thoughts would have been inconceivable to me a few years ago," she admits, "but today it would be impossible not to believe."

Certainly the most tragic of the circumstances surrounding Pat's residence on crooked Lombard Street was the mysterious death of her closest friend and secretary in one of the most mysterious fires ever investigated by the San Francisco Fire Department.

On June 20, 1969 a blaze unaccountably started in the master bedroom where Mary Louise Ward—who was discovered dead in bed after the fire—had been staying in Pat's absence. Firemen had difficulty entering the house for the front door was chained and barred from the inside. The possibility that Mary Louise had accidentally started the fire while smoking in bed was ruled out. She didn't smoke. That a guest might have been responsible also seemed unlikely, for the bedroom door was also *locked from the inside.*

Though an autopsy revealed that the victim was dead before the fire, the actual cause of her death was *not* determined. There was no evidence of heart failure, sedation or drunkeness. Mary Louise's internal organs were in good order and she had not suffocated. The investigation was finally dropped, the cause of death remaining a mystery.

Pat moved from the besieged townhouse but continued to be haunted by the experience. Concerned for the safety of the new tenants, she enlisted the aid of two mediums, Gerri Patton and Nick Nocerino. At her request, the two psychic investigators visited the house.

Though Nick knew nothing of its history, he was able to pick up psychically not only Pat's traumatic experiences but also those of previous tenants unknown to her. His impressions were specific, including names and details. Research on Pat's part revealed that the former residents had indeed been involved in a series of tragic events that resulted in divorce, great personal loss and/or suicide.

The strangest incident connected with the investigation involved photographs taken by Nocerino inside the house. These revealed weird light configurations, despite the *absence* of artificial lights (light bulbs, flash bulbs, chandeliers or cut glass, etc.) with their capacity for reflection. Some prints clearly show a woman bending over a drawer with one hand raised as though in surprise at some discovery. The image was not on the negative and there was no one in the room at the time except Nick who was taking the pictures.

In an effort to verify the authenticity of the prints, Pat arranged to have the negatives developed again under laboratory conditions with five independent witnesses present. The freshness of the chemicals was determined, negatives were brushed with a static free brush, the time of the exposure was recorded and every step of the developing process observed by all. Shapes appeared on the prints that were not on the negative and several looked as though light was coming from some unknown source. The same ghostly face and figure of a woman was again clearly visible although no such person had been seen or intentionally photographed in the haunted townhouse. Since the whole roll had been shot there, there seemed no possibility of a double exposure.

Hoping to avert more tragedy, Nocerino performed an exorcism on the house. "It was difficult to bring myself to give validity to such an act," Pat admitted to me, "and yet, I no longer feel uneasy about the place. Everything now appears to be stable and normal."

One can only hope.

Pat Montandon
Photo by Fran Ortiz,
courtesy of California Living Magazine

69

Peninsula School

A bride dead under mysterious circumstances. A grand mansion built at great cost and then abandoned.

The legend begins here and then twists and turns into a dark labyrinth of possibilities. The impressive structure (Peninsula Way, Menlo Park) built by San Mateo County Assemblyman James Coleman in 1880 cost $100,000—a fantastic sum in those days. According to one nostalgic story it was to be a gift for his lovely wife, the former Carmelita Nuttall, a woman described by contemporary newspapers as "peerless in beauty and accomplishments."

The mansion was nearing completion when a tragic event occurred that cast a somber shadow over the place for nearly one hundred years. Coleman returned from a business trip to the San Francisco hotel suite that he shared with Carmelita. Though it was 5 a.m., the dutiful young wife rose from bed and proceeded to unpack his bags. Somehow, as she was removing a gun from his valise, Carmelita accidentally shot herself.

It's said that the distraught bridegroom never set foot in the Peninsula palace that had only just been completed. The house changed hands several times over the years, no one lingering long. In 1906, a young woman is said to have ended her life there, hurling herself headlong down a steep stairway.

When the founders of the Peninsula School purchased the mansion in 1925, they acquired a resident ghost as well. Almost from the beginning Carmelita Coleman was a loved (and feared) member of the school community. The romantic tradition of her tenancy has grown with the years, sparked by some very vivid experiences.

Yesterday's Victorian elegance has been replaced by today's space age funk at the Coleman place but the legend of Carmelita is still very real. For more than fifty years there have been stories of shimmering lights, unexplained footstep and pets that refused to enter the building. Generations of children have told of glimpsing the wraithlike figure of a woman dressed in green. Some say the woman herself is green. Once an entire class saw the apparition.

Ken Coale, a former caretaker, remembers quite vividly being awakened at 3 a.m. one summer morning by the sound of footsteps. "I had been sleeping on a couch in the staff room," he recalls. "The footsteps seemed to come from the room just above me on the second floor. I lay there absolutely petrified." Finally Coale forced himself to track the sounds. They grew louder and louder as he climbed the stairs.

Then just as he reached the landing a door opened before him. He entered and the door closed behind him. The room from which the footsteps had seemingly come was empty. The only window was closed. Opening it, Coale looked down. It was a forty foot drop to the ground below and there was no indication of anyone having taken that exit. The house was quiet now. Whoever or whatever had been there was gone.

Mary Anne Collins, a parent of a Peninsula student and a one-time custodian, felt Carmelita's presence many times but never actually saw her.

Joe Starr and Monique Caine, teachers at Peninsula, tell of an overnight at the school when some twenty children saw an apparition. Starr described the vision as a green woman who appeared to be transparent. As he attempted to approach the figure it moved backward but remained visible for a full five minutes. Starr asked the children to sketch what they had seen and found that all the drawings were similar—a green woman who seemed to shimmer.

Starr encountered the apparition another night. This time the green lady confronted him in a black hallway when he was all alone. He flipped the light switch, but nothing happened. Man and ghost stared at one another for a few very long moments. Then the vision simply disappeared.

Many of the students are quite blase about their ghost. "I see it all the time," Shawn Kelman told an interviewer. "She's green." Panos Koutsoyannis told of "running through it"—to the amazement of a group of playmates.

Barney Young, director of the school, believes the ghost to be a benevolent one, pointing out that no one has ever been hurt by it. "The green lady has a way of taking hold of us. Kids may start out by being rather skeptical. 'I don't believe in that kind of stuff,' a newcomer will say. I always think to myself, 'Just ask him about the ghost in another year, after he's been here at night some time. That's enough to make a believer of anyone.' Often kids will say, 'Come quick. There's the ghost!' Teachers think they're being put on until they see it too."

Anna Mary Peck, who researched the Peninsula School for a study in folklore in 1973, found mystical significance in the very greenness of the ghost. In ancient heraldry, green symbolized eternal life, youth and hope—very appropriate for an old school ghost.

A decorator's nightmare, but a child's delight, the Peninsula School was the site of the movie, *Escape from Witch Mountain.* If houses can be typecast—this one was a natural.

In June of 1976 a seance was held at the school. In the presence of some fifty people, a voice speaking through the San Francisco medium Macelle Brown introduced herself as the original owner and related a heretofore untold tale of an unhappy marriage, a lover, a very jealous husband and a murder—her own.

Then, to everyone's surprise, another ghost "came through" claiming to be Carmelita's father, R. R. Nuttall, but dismissing her story as "hogwash."

"Why shouldn't I be here?" he demanded to know. "It was my money that built the place, not Coleman's." Nuttall then explained that he visits the school from time to time to note the modern improvements and watch the students. He enjoys children, likes progress, has no messages and wishes no one ill.

What really happened?

How will we ever know when even the ghosts themselves can't get their stories straight?

The Rengstorff House

Rising in eerie silence amid the lonely marshlands east of Mountain View is the Rengstorff mansion (1737 Stierlin Road). It was once a showplace, but its windows are now boarded up. Whether this is to keep the living out or the dead in nobody's quite certain.

The ornate structure—a montage of Gothic and Victorian architecture complete with widow's walk and classical columns—has stood vacant since the mid-1960's, a ghostly reminder of a colorful past.

The old house, now vandalized and dilapidated, was built in 1887 by Henry Rengstorff, a German immigrant who amassed a fortune farming and shipping grain, and became one of the founding fathers of Mountain View. Six children were born and grew up there in apparent happy prosperity. In 1906, Rengstorff, who had arrived in this country with only four dollars in his pocket, died in the house—a very wealthy man.

Shortly afterward, Perry Askam, the Rengstorff's orphaned grandson, came to live at the family house. Askam grew up to be a successful Broadway singing star, appearing in many popular musicals of his day. In 1945 he and his wife returned to the Rengstorff home. Once again the place was a social mecca. Between concert appearances with the San Francisco Symphony Orchestra, the Askams entertained lavishly. The gala era ended with Askam's death in 1961.

The house was then acquired by the Newhall Development Company and a series of disputes began. Should the place be demolished, relocated or refurbished? For nearly twenty years historians, developers and city politicians have hotly debated the issue; while within the house itself a different sort of energy has made itself felt.

A series of tenants and neighbors have reported unexplainable manifestations—the sound of crying late at night, lights that flash on and off, uncanny cold drafts. During the many vacant periods, passersby have reported seeing a young woman with long hair standing in the upstairs window staring out at the marshland below.

During the early 1960's Max and Mayetta Crump lived in the house. Crump was at that time manager of the Newhall Land and Farming Co., and part of his pay included the right to live in the Rengstorff mansion. For a time the Crumps and their two young sons lived uneventfully in the house, then they began to hear thumping noises on the stairs. Crump bought fly paper which he placed on the steps. Though they continued to hear noises, the fly paper was undisturbed.

During the night Mr. and Mrs. Crump would be awakened by a child crying, but upon investigation they would find their children sound asleep. They decided to move the whole family into one room at night, but the sounds of crying in other parts of the house continued.

Crump then borrowed a rifle specially sighted for night use. Night after night he sat up watching for whatever might appear. Nothing ever did though the noises continued.

During their three-year tenancy, the Crumps eliminated the possibility of an animal in the house, for the fly paper was never disturbed nor were there any other traces ever found. The theory of a human practical joker was also discarded.

"Finally I just came to believe that there was something in the house that I couldn't understand," Crump admitted in later years to Robert I. Pack who was investigating the house for the *Palo Alto Times*.

Though the Crumps grew used to their unseen house-mates, friends did not. Once a couple dropped by when the Crumps were out. While the husband was standing before the front door, the knob turned. His wife could see into the house from a large window at the side.

It was empty.

Adding to the mystery was a set of restraining cuffs which were among the furnishings within the house when the Crumps moved in. No one knows what part they may have played in the long forgotten history of the old mansion.

The debate of what to do with the Rengstorff place continues as the vandalized home remains vacant of human inhabitants. Numerous schemes have been formulated over the years. Most recently the three persons later convicted of the Chowchilla school bus kidnapping case reportedly made plans to acquire the house. Efforts ended abruptly with their arrest. Talk now centers around moving the mansion to Mountain View's Shoreline Park.

One wonders . . . if the house goes—will the ghost go with it?

Wheeler Office

Webster defines the poltergeist as "a mischievous ghost held to be responsible for unexplained noises."

This prosaic definition hardly describes the pandemonium that has terrorized homeowners, theater goers, patrons of bars, hotels, bakeries and even used car lots. It doesn't mention the variety of smells that have pleased or sickened witnesses and can't begin to convey the horror of finding oneself choked by unseen hands or the sight of sudden bursts of flame, flying knives or falling stones.

Students of the phenomena have attempted to explain poltergeists in one of three ways: earthbound spirits, energy caused by suppressed frustrations, or the devil.

It was a very bad day at the office for members of George H. Wheeler's court reporting firm, who finally gave up the business as usual pretense on June 16, 1964 and called police to their office on Franklin Street in Oakland. It was fervently hoped by all that the long arm of the law could reach into the realm of the supernatural.

After several weeks of bedlam that defied explanation, they had come to believe that their otherwise ordinary office had been targeted by poltergeist forces. Whether earthbound spirits, suppressed frustrations or the devil—they wanted them OUT.

What happened still remains a mystery to those involved, but Dr. Arthur Hastings, a University of California parapsychologist, developed some very provocative theories.

When asked to investigate the case, he soon discovered a strange set of circumstances. Early in January a twenty-year-old man had been employed by the firm as a typist. He was apparently liked by all but treated somewhat as a child. "There's no doubt that he was low man on the totem pole and knew it," Hastings explained to me.

"A few weeks later phones began to ring for no reason. Once answered, there was no one on the line. The ringing would then begin again so quickly that there was no time for an outside prankster to dial, wait for an answer, hang up and dial again," Hastings says. "This began in February. By March the calls had increased so that it became impossible for anyone to call the office because the lines were constantly busy, yet no one was calling out.

"Every telephone had to be replaced, although the phone company was positive that each was in perfect working order. Once this had been accomplished, the mysterious calls stopped."

Unfortunately this was only the beginning. All at once typewriter springs began to break. As fast as Joseph Morrow, the typewriter repairman, would fix one machine, another would suddenly break. Mystified, Morrow could find no cause for such an occurrence. The machines were mostly new, had always been serviced regularly and until that time had worked perfectly.

James Ambrosia, the city electrical building inspector, was called and gave the office a thorough going over. He could find nothing wrong—electrically speaking.

Next, coffee cups began to blow up and bulky six-foot cabinets tipped over for no reason. Framed plaques and pictures flew off the wall and a ceramic vase shot seven feet from a closet shelf across the room before crashing to the floor.

By this time everyone in the office was certain that the young employee was the culprit, for the disturbances invariably occurred in his presence. At the same time, they were all in agreement that he was doing nothing manually to cause them.

Another strong indication of his guilt became apparent when the young man would leave the office, located on the third floor of a large building, to visit acquaintances on other floors. The phenomena went with him, occurring everywhere that he went. Meanwhile back in the court reporting office, peace and quiet prevailed.

"Surprisingly there was very little animosity directed toward the man," Hastings says. "Though all agreed that he was causing the problems that were literally destroying the office and most accepted the theory of pent up hostilities somehow triggering the violence, they remained tolerant. It was as though they, themselves, somehow assumed a portion of the responsibility. It was a kind of family situation with all the implicit characteristics of conflict, punishment and forgiveness inherent in such a relationship."

The young man was allowed to take his typing home. Immediately the troubles stopped. When he returned, they began again. The pattern continued until the inevitable publicity brought the police into the case.

"After hours of questioning, the man confessed and was arrested and almost immediately released," Hastings says. "No one—probably not even the police—took the confession seriously. To have tipped over a large filing cabinet in the presence of six people without their awareness would have been difficult in the extreme. Yet somehow the arrest and public atonement satisfied some need. Though his job remained open to him, the young man insisted upon quitting. He has not been heard from again. It is unlikely he will be.

What could he possibly do for an encore?

The Easkoot House

Surely the most ghostly ghost around is Captain Alfred Easkoot, who wanders the misty shores of Marin on stormy nights searching, searching, searching for his golden hook.

In life, Easkoot had a withered hand to which a golden hook was fixed. In death, as his casket was carried across the sand, the hook somehow became detached and was washed out to sea.

It would be hard to find a more classic example of folk fantasy and yet there are many over the years who claim to have seen the shadowy form of the old sea captain silhouetted against the dunes of Stinson Beach. Still more have testified to poltergeist phenomena in the captain's now deserted house.

Captain Easkoot's lumber schooner went aground one hundred years ago on Duxbury Reef. He survived the wreck and built a house from the remnants that washed ashore. There he lived alone and apparently content until he fell in love. How the crusty old salt managed to woo and wed a beautiful and elegant woman with the romantic name of Amelia is another mystery, but he did.

The captain's snug cabin was torn down and redesigned to suit the taste of his eastern bride. (The original ship's timbers may still be seen in the stairway of the graceful New England Colonial.)

The tragedy is that only a short while later Amelia died, leaving Easkoot alone once more—but no longer happy with his solitary lot.

Easkoot never recovered from his loss, mourning Amelia until his own death many years later. As time passed he became embittered. The once proud manor house was allowed to fall into disrepair until almost obscured by vines and bushes. Easkoot took to roaming the beaches with a spyglass watching for ships and potential trespassers.

Competition developed between Easkoot and Nathan Stinson—the Point Reyes dairy farmer for whom the town is named—for the area's seashore business. The rivalry became an obsession that absorbed Easkoot until his death in 1905. That his home would eventually become the property of a Stinson—Eve Stinson Fitzhenry—seems the final irony.

The house enjoyed a brief renaissance during Mrs. Fitzhenry's ownership in the 1930s. Charming gardens were planted and groves of trees that have now grown tall, totally concealing the house and blocking the sea view as well. It was during this period that stories began to circulate concerning the place. Doors opened and closed of their own volition. Lights flashed on and off of their own accord. There were unexplainable cold spots and smells. Tales were told of the shadowy figure of a man with a loose dangling sleeve and a seaman's cap. The house was sold and resold, changing hands several times. The residence of the most recent tenants terminated abruptly when the house caught fire.

That morning in March of 1976 great clouds of smoke were seen pouring from the house. The blaze gutted parts of the interior, blackened the outside and destroyed thousands of dollars worth of antiques and paintings. Fortunately no one was in the house at the time. Rumors are rampant but the official fire report, accepted by the insurance company, lists the cause as a defective electric heater. Though many belongings remain about the charred house, the tenants did not return. Their whereabouts are unknown.

And so the legend continues. It's easy to imagine that the misanthropic captain continues to view trespassers with hostility. Though the property is beautiful, the lovely house restorable, the For Sale sign remains.

At night when the fog shrouds the coast and whitecaps dot the swirling surf, lights may flicker inside the abandoned house. "Maybe it's the captain," someone invariably suggests.

And who's to say he's wrong?

Mother Lode Country

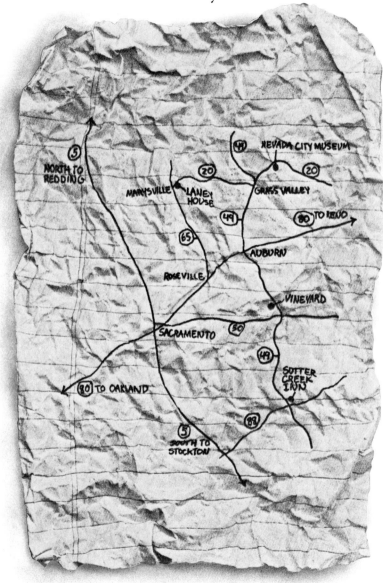

Nevada County Historical Museum

"The equipment of the Nevada County Fire Department is not to be excelled by that of any similar organization in any town of the same size on the Pacific Slope. The town is well supplied with hydrants and the water pressure is strong enough to throw a stream over the highest buildings."

The *Nevada City Transcript* had good reason to boast that March morning in 1877. A well equipped fire department meant life itself to the tinderbox towns of the Mother Lode.

Firehouse No. 1 had been built in 1861. The Victorian bell tower and gingerbread trim were added a few years later. The facility continued in use until 1938. Ten years later it was converted into a museum by the Nevada County Historical Society.

But the excitement was by no means over. As the antiques and artifacts arrived—so did something else. Something with an ornery desire to push people around.

Hjalmer E. Berg, director of the museum, reports inexplicable footsteps and cold air currents. "Many times I've been alone in the museum but known that I wasn't alone," he says.

Once Rebecca Miller, president of the historical society, tried to shut a cabinet door. "As fast as I could close the door, it would fly back open," she recalls. "Finally I said aloud, 'Stop this, I don't have time!' It stopped, but then I heard footsteps behind me. I turned, but there was no one there." (Surely a classic case of a ghost having the last word.)

Berg tells of a time when a Jesuit priest and two graduate students were touring the otherwise empty museum. They ascended the stairs to the second floor and returned almost immediately. "Are you playing a joke on us?" the priest asked. It seemed that a redhaired "floozy" in old

Hjalmer E. Berg

fashioned finery had startled them by appearing out of nowhere, sitting down at the piano—a relic from an old whorehouse—and beginning to plink away.

"It didn't help at all to tell him that we had no such woman employed at the museum—which, of course, we don't. The idea of a spectral volunteer was even more alarming than a prostitute."

Another time a group of Business and Professional Women were visiting the museum. They'd examined everything on the first level and had just climbed the stairs to the second floor when all of a sudden one woman began to scream. "They're after me!" she shrieked, running down the stairs and out the front door. No one was ever able to learn what had frightened her so."

One of the most interesting features within the museum is an 1880 photograph of an Irish miner named Carrigan. The subject is a mature, white-bearded man, but to the side of the photograph is the image of a boy of about twelve.

According to the story, Carrigan told the astonished photographer that as the picture was taken he was thinking rather nostalgically of his boyhood. It would seem that these thoughts somehow transmitted themselves to the film, emerging as his own youthful countenance. As the years pass the boy seems to be growing clearer. Some see other faces in the photograph as well.

Nick Nocerino says these other faces are Chinese ghosts. Nick came to the museum at Berg's request to exorcise the place when the phenomena seemed to be taking on a more hostile character.

Both men believed that the evil influence was emanating from the thousand-year-old Taoist shrine at one end of the museum. The shrine had been taken from a Grass Valley joss house—joss meaning god—and is believed to be the oldest of its kind in North America.

As visitors to the museum stood in front of the shrine, many experienced the sensation of being pushed or shoved. Some said they felt as if someone was trying to trip them.

Attendance at the museum was dwindling and Berg—proud of the historic displays he'd worked so hard to accumulate—was concerned.

Nick was able to tune in psychically to the situation, making contact with two Chinese spirits who admitted that they had been tripping pagans who got too close to their sacred altar.

Nick performed an exorcism ceremony to dispatch the ghosts. Berg put up a rail to discourage the guests. Between the two of them, everything's back to normal at the museum.

The Sutter Creek Inn

The Sutter Creek Inn is alive with ghosts—both nice and naughty.

Not only does the house—a New England clapboard—attract phenomena, so does its owner, Jane Way.

Jane bought the house in 1966. "Just why, I can't imagine," she says today. "It was an all time low in my life. My son had been killed in an accident. My husband and I had just split. My health was terrible—I'd had cancer twice. I was feeling very, very sorry for myself."

Soon after while passing through San Francisco, she stopped on an impulse at a spiritualist church. "It was a crazy thing to do," she admits. "I was just driving down a street looking for an on-ramp to the freeway and saw the sign. I'd never been there before, never had known anyone who had—but suddenly there I was parking my car and walking in.

"The minister was Florence Becker, a very gifted medium. We'd never met before. Of course she couldn't know a thing about me—and yet she seemed to know everything. 'You've just lost your son,' she said almost immediately and then began to describe him in detail. Her description was so accurate that I began to cry.

"'You've bought an old place in the mountains,' she continued. 'I see people coming and going—it must be a hotel. That's right for you—but you must stop the bitterness. It could ruin everything for you. Keep on with what you're doing but without bitterness. You'll be successful.'"

Jane left the church and drove back to Sutter Creek. Again and again her mind returned to the medium's words. Then a few nights later she saw her first ghost.

"It was Saturday evening and all the hotel guests were out. I was getting ready to leave also; some friends were having a costume party. Suddenly I felt conscious of being watched and looked up. There was a tall man wearing old fashioned-looking clothes standing in the doorway. For a moment I thought he must be going to the same party. Then I heard the words: *I will protect your inn.* He smiled and then faded away.

"Well, really, how could I be bitter after an experience like that? Surely somebody out of this world had decided to take an interest in my affairs. What more could anyone ask? I suppose what had bothered me most was the apparent futility of life, its seeming transience. Now here in my own house was living proof of the continuity of the human spirit."

Jane believes that this was the spirit of State Senator Edward Convers Voorhies who had lived in the house for many years.

The house had originally been built in 1860 by John Keyes as a home for his young bride, Clara McIntire. It was hoped the New England lines would ease the loneliness for her native New Hampshire. The couple had one child who died of diphtheria when still a baby. Then in 1875 Keyes died leaving Clara a widow at thirty-four.

Two years later Voorhies came to town and proceeded to court her. They were married on March 29, 1880. The couple had two children. Earl died in infancy, but Gertrude lived to be ninety.

"I bought the house from Gertrude just before she moved to a rest home," Jane explains. "She'd lived in the place all her life and was very attached to it. I suppose that's why her spirit returned one evening during a seance that guests were holding in the livingroom—to check on things."

Jane's experience with Senator Voorhies, following so soon after the psychic reading, seems to have triggered a latent medium-ship within herself. In the intervening years she's experienced a wide variety of psychic phenomena.

"There was the German ophthalmologist who tried to help me with an eye problem. He didn't—but I know his intentions were good," she says.

Jane's less certain about a spectral exhibitionist—a flasher. "He seemed very proud of his endowments," she recalls. "I think he'd been punished in some way in his life, possibly been mutilated. You'd think death would be the end of earthly hang-ups; but, if he's any indication, we take them with us.

"Once a cat was flung against the wall by an unseen force—possibly a ghost who doesn't like cats. They don't like garlic either. We've discovered that with our seances. If you don't like ghosts a good fettuccine should eliminate any chance of an encounter."

A very good remedy to keep in mind.

Jane Way

83

Laney House

Anita and Francis Laney live in a Marysville Victorian manor house that looks like a frosty pink wedding cake. The architectural confection seems the antithesis of the Charles Addams haunt—yet a whole family of spirits reside there.

The Laneys bought the place in 1962, little dreaming what was in store for them. "The previous owners had no contact whatsoever with anything supernatural," Anita says. "Three years passed uneventfully. Then we began to be aware of a presence in the house. I'd come in the back door and hear music. 'Who left the stereo on?' I'd wonder. The answer was—no one. The stereo wasn't on. The music was coming from another world.

"Then the Republican women wanted to have a tea at the house. I came home from the office to get the kitchen cleaned up for them. I was rushed and not in the best mood when I heard a man's footsteps behind me. I thought, 'Oh, hell!' certain that it was my husband wanting lunch.

" 'What are you doing here?' I asked without turning. There was no answer, yet I could *feel* someone standing just behind me. When I turned at last I found that the kitchen was empty."

One night Anita switched off the bedside lamp and settled back, only to be confronted by the head and shoulders of a man floating above the marble-topped dresser. She turned the light back on and it was gone, turned it off again and this time saw a full length form of a man.

"I knew exactly who it was," Anita says. "Norman Abbott Rideout—first owner of the house. I recognized him because he's a younger version of his father, Norman Danning Rideout, the prominent Gold Country banker of the last century—I'd seen *his* picture many times. I knew that the elder Rideout had built the house as a wedding gift for his son in 1885.

"Eleven years later the young husband and father was the sole victim in a mine disaster. I'm certain that it's this man whom I saw then and have seen again many times over the years."

The Laneys believe that the house is haunted not only by Norman but by his wife and their children as well. "We hear their voices and footsteps often and sometimes catch glimpses of them as well," Francis explains. "There's a little boy and a pretty little girl with long blond hair—she resembles her grandfather."

"Norman and his wife are very fashionably dressed," Anita adds. "She's quite beautiful. I see her standing at the window often. They seem like such a happy family. Maybe that's why they stay here; possibly they're living out the happy times they shared in this house. It reminds me of the ghost in *Our Town* who came back to relive one day. Maybe they've chosen to remain here for all eternity. That would be a kind of heaven, now wouldn't it?"

Footsteps are the most common phenomena experienced by the Laneys and their guests. One evening Anita was entertaining a branch of the American Association of University Women.

"We had just heard a review of the Edgar Cayce biography, *There Is a River,* and I was serving refreshments when we all heard the front door open," Anita recalls. "Guess the movie's out, sounds like Fran coming home," one woman said.

"But Fran didn't come in to say hello. Instead the steps went clomping on up the stairs. I called out to him and when he didn't answer I went to investigate. Nobody was there.

"Just a few minutes later a guest cried out as her spoon tore itself out of her hand and flew across the room. Somebody was there but it certainly wasn't Fran!"

The first time the Laneys heard spectral voices they were startled, but over the years have grown accustomed to them—with one exception. As Anita was bathing one morning, she heard a woman call out from downstairs. "Then a man's voice answered her—from right there in the bathroom," Anita says. "I leaped out of the tub and grabbed a towel. Ghost or no ghost, I didn't like the idea of a strange man in the bathroom with me!"

Anita believes that ghosts are keeping an eye on her in more ways than one. "They have their little ways of telling me they think I'm doing too much, getting involved in too many projects. One night—morning really, it was three a.m.—I was sitting on the floor surrounded by big rolls of newsprint. Though awfully tired, I felt obligated to complete a club assignment that I'd undertaken, a decorating project.

"I heard footsteps quite clearly descending the stairs. I thought it was Fran and I was so determined to finish that I didn't say a word. The steps reached the foot of the stairs, walked down the hall and across the livingroom. Finally they were right behind me. I turned at last and saw—no one. Well, when it gets so bad that a ghost has to come and tell you to slow down, you begin to get the message. I got up and went to bed."

The ghosts sometimes appear a bit like animals misbehaving when their humans are away. "Once a young couple were staying in the house while we were on vacation," Anita recalls. "While sitting in the livingroom, they heard a terrific crash upstairs. Upon investigating, they found that two tall vases and an antique compote had fallen off a shelf.

"Our young friends were terribly upset when we got back. 'We just can't explain it,' they kept saying. *I* could explain it well enough. I went right upstairs and said aloud, 'This doesn't please me at all. I'm very disappointed.' I left the pieces on the floor for six weeks as a kind of reminder. It hasn't happened again."

But co-existing with ghosts is a two-way street, Anita admits. "If we don't hear from them for a while, we get worried. What if they should go away! Sometimes I ask, 'Are you angry with me? I'm sorry if I've done anything to displease you.' Sometimes I've even pleaded, 'Come back!'

"And they always do."

The Vineyard House

Louise Allhoff must have been a hard woman to live with.

There was a first husband, a successful vintner, who committed suicide in a Virginia City outhouse.

Then along came Robert Chambers, the merchant prince of the Gold Rush capital, Coloma. Attracted to the beautiful widow with her easy elegance and proud, imperious ways, Chambers persuaded her to marry him.

For a time they were a formidable team. Chalmers had the hustle, Louise had the class. They enlarged her vineyards and won prizes for their wines. Chalmers was elected to the State legislature. While his financial empire continued to grow, she introduced "culture" to the area.

At the apex of their success, this pair of high rollers constructed a four-story mansion (Cold Spring Road and Highway 49) which was to be a mecca for the Mother Lode elite. Among the attractions of their "Vineyard House" was a ninety-foot ballroom and a music room.

But Robert Chalmers' pleasure was brief. Soon after completion of the showplace in 1878, his manner began to change. The former orator now talked in whispers. Seeing a grave being dug in the cemetery across the street, he walked over and laid down to see if it would fit him.

Soon—according to Louise—Chalmers was a raving maniac and she was forced to chain him in the cellar of their home. It was said that she came down often to taunt him, standing always just beyond his frenzied grasp. Chalmers' misery lasted for nearly three years. In 1881, he starved to death, fearing that Louise was trying to kill him.

Call it divine retribution or merely bad luck, hard times befell Louise. A blight attacked her grapes. The Chinese immigrants who slept in the vineyards to keep deer out were expelled in a pogrom and the remaining grapes ravaged by humans and animals. Their real estate holdings dwindled during Chalmers' illness and the bank foreclosed on the Vineyard House.

Louise was allowed to remain on a rent paying basis; but, in order to do so, was forced to take in roomers and to allow the cellar to be used as an auxiliary jail. At least two prisoners spent their last night on earth there. One was a school teacher who had killed a student, the other a highwayman. The teacher recited poetry from the scaffold, the highwayman danced a jig and then burst into tears.

Louise died, lonely and impoverished, in 1900. The proud mansion where Ulysses S. Grant once made a speech fell into melancholy decay as a series of owners came and went, always complaining of unaccountable sounds. One tenant left suddenly in the middle of the night, refusing to talk about what he'd seen.

In 1956 the house was turned into an inn and restaurant. Drinks are now served in the cellar jail where thieves and murderers once languished. Dave Vanbuskirk, one of the owners, has often heard unexplained steps on the stairs and seen a doorknob turn before his startled eyes—with no one on the other side. Once in the seemingly empty house a freshly made bed came unmade and the impression of a form could clearly be seen on the sheets. The fact that Vanbuskirk had, himself, found a stack of old coffins under the front porch shortly after buying the place did little to cheer him.

During the night guests have reported hearing the sound of chains rattling, rustling skirts, heavy breathing and brisk steps. One Sacramento couple heard a raucous group enter by the front door and climb the stairs laughing loudly. Going to the door to quiet the revelers, they saw three men dressed in Victorian clothing fade before their eyes.

Photo by C. J. Marrow

Bibliography

Master Ghost Chasers At Work

Taff, B.E. "Stalking the Elusive Spectre," *Probe,* October 1973.

Taff, Barry E. and Gaynor, Kerry. "A New Poltergeist Effect," *Theta, A Journal for Research on the Question of Survival After Death,* Vol. 4, No. 2, Spring 1976.

Taff, Barry E. and Gaynor, Kerry. "Another Wild Ghost Chase?: No, One Hell of a Haunt," The Neuropsychiatric Institute, UCLA Center for the Health Sciences.

Vance, Adrian. "UCLA Group Uses Camera To Hunt Ghosts," *Popular Photography,* May 1976.

San Diego Area

Buckley, Marcie. *The Crown City's Brightest Gem,* Hotel del Coronado, 1975.

Crane, Clare. "Jesse Shepard and the Villa Montezuma," *The Journal of San Diego History,* Summer 1970.

Davidson, Winifred. "Hanged for Boat-Stealing," *The San Diego Union,* October 6, 1935.

Davidson, Winifred. "They Blessed This Senorita," *The San Diego Union,* March 17, 1935.

Freeman, Don. "The Mocker," *Old West,* Winter 1973.

Holzer, Hans. *Ghosts of the Golden West,* Ace Books, 1968.

Perkins, Eloise. "Rancho Jamul Is Where It Happens," *Times-Advocate,* June 22, 1975.

Rice, Edna Taft. *A Clairvoyant Approach to Haunting,* California Parapsychology Foundation, Inc., 1968.

Reading, June A. *The Thomas Whaley House,* Historical Shrine Foundation of San Diego County, 1960.

Los Angeles Area

Hyams, Joe. "Our Haunted House," *Reader's Digest,* November 1966.

Hyams, Joe. "The Day I Gave Up the Ghost," *Saturday Evening Post,* June 3, 1967.

Moss, Thelma and Schmeidler, Gertrude. "Quantitative Investigation of a 'Haunted House' with Sensitives and a Control Group," *Journal of the American Society for Psychical Research,* Vol. 62, No. 4, October 1968.

Northrop, Marie E. "The Yorba Family Cemetery: California's Oldest," *National Genealogical Society Quarterly,* Vol. 57, No. 2, June 1969.

Central California

Beck, Larry. "Pacheco Pass," The Nirvana Foundation

Guthertz, Alvin T. "How A Publicity Stunt Turned Up A Ghost," *Psychic World,* September 1976.

Rambo, Ralph. *Lady of Mystery,* The Rosicrucian Press, 1967.

Reinstedt, Randall A. *Ghosts, Bandits & Legends of Old Monterey,* Ghost Town Publications, 1974.

San Francisco Area

Asbury, Herbert. *The Barbary Coast*, Garden City Publishing Company, Inc., 1933.

Atherton, Gertrude. *Adventures of a Novelist*, Liveright, 1932.

Butler, Phyllis Filiberti. *The Valley of Santa Clara, Historic Buildings, 1792-1920*, The Junior League of San Jose, Inc., 1975.

Chapman, Elizabeth. "I'll Take the Back Road," *Stockton Record*, May 8, 1964.

Landmarks Preservation Advisory Board, Revised Case Report, March 20, 1974, The Atherton House.

Landmark Proposal, San Francisco Art Institute.

Leonidas K. Haskell file, California State Historical Society.

McDonald, James M. "Recollections of Early Days in San Francisco," *Harper's Weekly*, October 22, 1859.

Mason, Jack, with Thomas Barfield. *Last Stage for Bolinas*, North Shore Books, 1973.

Montandon, Pat. *The Intruders*, Coward, McCann & Geoghegan, Inc., 1975.

Pack, Robert I. "Rengstorff Mansion Haunted? Whooo Knows?", *Palo Alto Times*, August 10, 1972.

Olmsted, Roger R. *Here Today*, Chronicle Books, 1968.

Peck, Anna Mary. "A Study in Folk Lore," unpublished, 1973.

Stern, Daniel K. "Guns of Destiny," *Westways*, February 1953.

"The Story of Fort Mason, Historic U.S. Army Post in San Francisco" prepared by the information office, U.S. Army Transportation Terminal Command, Pacific, Fort Mason, December 10, 1960.

Wallace, Kevin. "It's Haunted—But Home," *San Francisco Chronicle*, October 31, 1974.

Mother Lode Country

Centennial Issue—1877-1977, Nevada County Historical Society.

Grieg, Michael. "A Psychic Prober Exorcises Ghosts," *San Francisco Chronicle*, February 4, 1974.

Miscellaneous

Caughey, John W. *California*, Prentice-Hall, 1953.

Haining, Peter. *Ghosts*, Macmillan Publishing Co., Inc. 1975.

Hoover, Mildred Brooke; Rensch, Ethel; Rensch, Hero. *Historic Spots in California*, Stanford University Press, 1966.

Mitchell, Edgar. *Psychic Explorations, a Challenge to Science*, Putnam, 1974.

Nava, Julian and Barger, Bob. *California*, Glencoe Press, 1976.

Newcomb, Rexford. *The Old Missions and Historic Homes of California*, J. B. Lippincott Company, 1925.